The Connecticon

Learning for the Connected Generation

Frank Rennie

and

Robin Mason

INFORMATION AGE
PUBLISHING

80 Mason Street • Greenwich, Connecticut 06830 • www.infoagepub.com

Library of Congress Cataloging-in-Publication Data

Mason, Robin.
  The connecticon : learning for the connected generation / Robin Mason
and Frank Rennie.
     p. cm.
  Includes bibliographical references.
  ISBN 1-59311-209-2 (pbk.) – ISBN 1-59311-210-6 (hardcover)
  1. Education–Effect of technological innovations on. 2. Internet in
education. I. Rennie, Frank. II. Title.
  LB1028.3.M382 2004
  371.33'44678–dc22

                                                        2004020287

Printed in the United States of America

CONTENTS

Preface

Our aim in writing this book is to bring together evidence from a range of fields that suggests there is a profound change happening in the nature of learning. The level and degree of this change is such that we have only been able to provide a snap shot, based primarily on our own interests and experience. Many other aspects could have been analysed and developed. We do not claim to have covered the extent of this change comprehensively or to have researched the various components in the depth we would have liked. We have aimed to raise awareness and to juxtapose ideas, issues and evidence from several domains in order to provide an initial scoping of the territory. We have avoided using 'new paradigm' terminology as unhelpful to our aim, but have perhaps fallen into a worse trap of coining a new word: the Connecticon. We have done this as a way of highlighting the significance of the change and of conceptualising the notion that the processes, the content and the means of knowing are no longer what they were even ten years ago.

It is important to stipulate that this change is not entirely or overwhelmingly positive. We have tried to indicate some of the losses, the dangers and the dilemmas that these changes are producing. Ignoring the changes or simply decrying them does not constitute a solution however, and we try to indicate proactive responses based on the understanding that these changes are profound, fundamental and far reaching.

No doubt there will be objections to the case we have tried to make about the impact of these changes: that enthusiasts have overhyped the impact of the web; that we know little about the processes of learning, so how can we claim it is radically altered; that every generation likes to think that it is on the cusp of profound change as a form of self promotion, and so on. More serious objectors will point to lack of research evidence, the scatter-gun approach we have adopted or the raising of issues without addressing them in depth. We acknowledge these shortcomings. Further research is certainly called for in understanding the effects of connected learning, both formal and informal, both short term and longer term, and both individual and personalised, and collaborative and technology-mediated. If readers are sufficiently moved to contact us, we would welcome correspondence on other examples of how the Connecticon is manifesting and how learning is affected. We will collect such evidence and make it available from our home pages:

www.lews.uhi.ac.uk/research/StaffRec1.htm

or

iet.open.ac.uk/pp/r.d.mason

We have used a cartoon at the beginning of each chapter to provide a different view and a lighter touch to the change agenda. We would like to thank the cartoonists: David Austin (chapter 2), Randy Glasbergen (chapters 1, 5, 7 and 10), Sidney Harris (chapters 6 and 8), Patricia Madigan (chapter 9) and Robert Thompson (chapters 3 and 4) for giving us permission to reproduce their delightfully provocative and humorous cartoons.

We have not indicated individual authorship of chapters, though indeed we did write more or less alternate chapters. We maintain that this was a truly collaborative venture in which our individual styles and viewpoints have melded.

—Robin Mason and Frank Rennie
June 2004

CHAPTER 1

The Connected Generation

After all our online chats,
it's great to finally
meet you in person.

Same here.

© 2000 Randy Glasbergen.

I t is the contention of this book that the Information Age has given way to a new paradigm: that of connection. Why do we need to invent a new word—*Connecticon*—to describe a simple and familiar concept? The following chapters are our attempt to answer this question, but at the outset it is

The Connecticon: Learning for the Connected Generation, pages 1–15

enough to say that the nature of the phenomenon is multi-varied and more conceptual than the commonplace term "connection" conveys. For example, consider the impact of the mobile phone on one-to-one communication: the way in which it has become indispensable to making physical connections with people at large gatherings, shopping trips, train and plane rendezvous and even at crowded discos and leisure events. Aside from these time and energy saving uses, the mobile phone has come to serve many more subtle and apparently useless kinds of connection: we have all had the misfortune to be subjected to overhearing "content-free" conversations of other people using their mobiles to connect with their friends, family or work colleagues in crowded spaces. There is clearly no real information being exchanged; the call appears to be fulfilling a completely different purpose. Furthermore, the callers are oblivious to the people around them, so all-absorbing is the connection through the ether. Despite reminders to people at public events such as lectures and concerts to turn off their mobiles, the desire for connection seems to override etiquette. In fact, the always-on mobile has become, for some people, an extension of the self—a barely conscious desire to be connected to a bigger world. The focus for our attention is imperceptibly changing and connectivity is at the heart of this evolution. Some social commentators consider that we are now living in an "attention economy," and we discuss this concept later in the chapter.

The change in attitude to telephony has taken place, in the UK at least, with remarkable speed. In the late 1980s and early 1990s, the UK Open University (OU) introduced online tutoring to large numbers of its students, and this required the use of a modem connected to the telephone line. The early evaluations of the impact of this technology on students' lives and study patterns indicated that the cost of the telephone calls was a major inhibitor to its take-up. The University went to great lengths to provide local-call dial-up service across most of the country (though even local calls are charged by the minute) and designed an off-line working front-end to the communications software, so great was the concern about students' reticence to use the phone for anything more than strategic calls for help. Interviews were carried out with students in their homes and data was collected on the actual costs of their calls over the period of their studies. In some cases these costs for the whole nine months of study amounted to no more than the price of a round of drinks in the pub (Mason, 1989). Of course, the habit of spending money in the pub was long-standing, while the traditionally telephone-shy British public found spending a similar sum on communication—especially where the benefits were more diffuse than simple information exchange—hard to swallow. Needless to say, the intervening years have seen an explosion of online communication in the OU, as elsewhere in higher education, and close to a million messages are exchanged every day by staff and the 300,000 OU students.

Despite this apparently rapid uptake of online communication in higher education, it is undoubtedly true that universities are at the trailing edge of the Connecticon. Young people are already inhabiting the connected economy and e-commerce initiatives are scrambling to provide community-friendly features on their websites. Just as semi-clad beauty queens were used to sell automobiles, now social spaces are big business on the net. Amazon.com uses customers to write personal views about their books and music; online games connect players to form temporary teams against the alien forces; LandsEnd.com allows you to shop for clothes in the online company of other shoppers. This is a more diffuse form of connection than the one-to-one intimacy of the mobile phone. It is human companionship or connection with people—never to be known or contacted personally—who are doing the same thing at the same time.

At the other end of the online connection spectrum, there are a vast range of chat rooms, support groups and discussion forums where getting to know the participants, sharing intimacies and building a "sharing caring" environment has spawned compelling social networks. Many academic books and how-to manuals have appeared to document this phenomenon (Kim, 2000; Palloff & Pratt, 1999; Preece, 2002; Rheingold, 1994).

CONNECTING PEOPLE ONLINE

A number of social commentators have pointed out that the Web has become a "town square" for community exchange in something of the same way that physical town squares used to function:

> As a society we're working harder, juggling more roles, and spending more of our free time at home—exhausted from our multifaceted lives, fearful of the violence that we see in movies, TV and video games, and physically removed from our family, friends and neighbors. So we go online—to shop, play games, trade collectibles, argue politics, or just shoot the breeze. The Web is becoming our collective town square—more and more, people are turning to Web communities to get their personal, social and professional needs met. (Kim, 2000, p. xi)

The extent to which people connecting online can be considered a community will be explored in detail in Chapter Two. It is sufficient here merely to note that online community is not without problems, for all that the participants may be communicating from the "safety" of their own homes.

As with all aspects of the profound changes that the Connecticon implies, there are gains and there are losses. Understanding the benefits without losing sight of the difficulties is our intention.

> The outcomes are not uniformly positive or negative. The new opportunities and constraints online interaction creates are double-edged, leading to results that can amplify both beneficial and noxious social processes. (Smith & Smith, 1999, p. 4)

Is the Connecticon simply about the formation of online groups, and the ability to connect disparate people who want to shop, play or chat with someone? In short, is it just about people connecting? No, this would be a surface level view of the situation and would not account for the impact of the previous Information Age. The telephone network would be adequate if the new paradigm were simply about connecting people. In fact, as we see, phones are evolving to include facilities to connect people to information and to other people around information. Personal Digital Assistants (PDAs) and pagers are further examples of connection devices, and even the television set is no longer simply a one-to many connection device.

> The personal handheld device market is poised to take the kind of jump that the desktop PC made between 1980 and 1990, from a useful toy adopted by a subculture to a disruptive technology that changes every aspect of society. (Rheingold, 2002, p. xv)

CONNECTING PEOPLE AND INFORMATION

In simple terms the Connecticon is a new way of looking at connected information communities as illustrated in Figure 1.1. The Connecticon is constructed of three layers, or elements, that interact constructively to give results that are extremely flexible, often unpredictable, and are innovative in an almost infinite variety of combinations—the ideal environment in fact to foster the culture of entrepreneurialism in business, education, and in society as a whole. The first layer of the Connecticon is the physical infrastructure of the Internet, the terminals, servers, cabling, routers and all the growing network of paraphernalia commonly known as cyberspace. Evidence shows us that this physical structure of the Internet is increasing at an enormous rate, and despite concerns about the digital gap, is truly global in its proportions.

This brings us on to the second layer of the Connecticon, which is the human resource located at the end of each terminal and node in this physical network. Many nodes have more than a single user, but even single users are enormously complicated repositories of knowledge, culture,

THE CONNECTICON

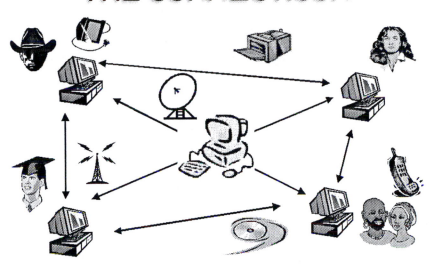

Figure 1.1.   The Connecticon.

behavior, and potential links to other value systems. This vast human resource, added to the physical network of cyberspace is a source for learning and innovation of gigantic proportions, even and possibly because of its unstructured state.

With the third layer of the Connecticon the potential for education and innovation grows exponentially in exciting and unpredictable ways, constrained only by the mathematical probability of serendipity. The third layer is the level of high quality, high speed interactions, both between users of the network, and between differing types of devices physically comprising the network—what we have termed hyper-interactivity. When we consider these three complex layers as part of an organic structure, not simply consisting of geographically isolated academics using computer terminals, but all types of people, young and old, communicating by computer, mobile phone, digital cameras, satellite and wireless communication links, geographical positioning systems, and with access to almost unbelievably large data storage facilities, then we can perhaps just begin to comprehend the potential of the Connecticon.

The Web forms the mixing bowl and takes the mixture into a virtual format that has a more tenuous relationship with time and space. Ubiquity, speed and global scale provide the heat to cook this into something we have not tasted before. All the ingredients are familiar but the process of transformation has produced a new paradigm. It is the aim of this book to identify and document the Connecticon—its nature, its impact and its implications. We will do this in the broad domain of learning, though a similar study could be carried out in commercial, social or political fields.

Learning in the Connecticon

Pedagogical theories and approaches have trends and fashions just as does the clothing industry. Within living memory we have seen the rise and fall of behaviourism, teaching machines, and educational television. To a large extent these approaches mirror social trends and try to exploit emerging technologies. In one sense, this is the role of education—to prepare students for participation in the prevailing social world, its economy and its technologies. If we agree that teaching and learning should change—albeit gradually—to reflect social values and needs, what changes are now required in the content and processes of learning in order to live and work in a Connecticon rather than an Information Age? Do we still want our children to be memorizing vast numbers of lines of poetry every year, as they used to a generation ago, or are there other skills, concepts and abilities we consider more useful, more appropriate and more in tune with the demands of a connected generation?

Learning to eLearn

Learning to learn has always been the Holy Grail of the education process and as such, always been more preached about than practised. The updated and arguably more urgently needed Holy Grail are the ability to elearn, that is, to learn to use the facilities and affordances of the online environment. It is more urgent in that the need to learn facts and information has vastly reduced and the ability to find, manipulate, analyse, synthesise and re-purpose information has increased concomitly. One of the key resources in developing these abilities is other people. Gone are the threats that machines will replace teachers; machines can store, link and process information, but people transform it and add value to it. Tutors, mentors and online facilitators are now seen as the asset that makes all the difference to student retention, motivation and acceptance of elearning. Likewise, CBT (computer-based training) put up on the Web with no human support, is increasingly seen as unsuccessful and a "horseless-carriage" use of connectivity (Reynolds et al., 2002). Because there is so much information available on the net, what is valued is knowing how to cope with it. Connecting with other people to share the load, to exchange tips and models for managing information, and to express ideas and give feedback, has become an essential element of elearning methodology. Belonging to a range of networks—some of which only connect online, while others avail themselves of whatever communication medium is most appropriate including face-to-face meetings—is an obvious strategy, up to a point, of increasing one's resources for managing information.

The influential 1994 study by Gibbons et al. (1994) drew a distinction between Mode 1 and Mode 2 forms of knowledge production. Mode 1 is characterised as propositional or codified knowledge, whereas Mode 2 knowledge is socially constructed and gives value to personal knowledge derived from application and problem-solving. Mode 2 forms of learning require participation in communities and depend on discussion, reflection and critique. This distinction has been somewhat overused and the dichotomy between the modes exaggerated. For example, Mode 1 has been associated with instructivist teaching where the teacher pours knowledge into the "empty head" of the student. Mode 2 has been linked to constructivist learning, where the teacher is a facilitator and even fellow learner. Mode 1 has been typified as "learning that," whereas Mode 2 is typified as "knowing how." In fact, neither mode exists in a pure form. Nevertheless, it is clear that Mode 2 approaches to learning are gaining greater acceptance and are certainly in tune with the environment created by the Connecticon.

Informal Learning

The idea of informal learning networks has a long pedigree, not least of which is the Folk High School movement (Glen, 1988). Now the corporate sector has begun to adopt the practices of informal learning and particularly in large, multinational organisations, to apply them to the online environment through support for distributed networks of employees across the company. There is a growing recognition that valuable learning often takes place in conversations, social interactions, and team projects, in which learning is part of the interactions between people. It has been acknowledged as one of the key reasons for forming communities of practice, networks, and other forums that allow people to network and socialize. Informal learning is not limited to a predefined body of knowledge, but rather emerges from the interaction of people. At the heart of it is the transfer of tacit knowledge—knowledge that is not articulated but is acquired by individuals through experience.

With increasingly distributed working environments, online collaborative learning spaces provide a container for interactions and relationships to develop, as those are the basis of informal learning. The Internet and groupware products must be seen as the medium for relationship creation, not information exchange. While there are undoubtedly disadvantages in the loss of face-to-face interaction, the advantages of developing the virtual informal learning dimension can free people from reactions to physical appearance, allow introverts to be "heard" in the conversation, and can provide a level playing field for interaction between managers and workers. Because in a collaborative learning space the conduits for learning are the central goal, there can be a straightforward exploration of multiple perspectives.

Assessment of eLearning

It is a disturbing paradox that higher education is becoming increasingly draconian about students plagiarising on assignments when the ability to find and re-purpose information is one of the very elearning skills that is increasingly valued elsewhere. Instead of developing software detection systems to identify paragraphs which students have cut and pasted from elsewhere into their assignments, surely a re-conceptualising of the nature of assessment would be much more appropriate. Of course buying assignments on the Web and claiming whole essays written by someone else as one's own are practices which should not be tolerated, but with thoughtful analysis of what the real learning outcomes of a course are—or should be—it is possible to so integrate the assessment into the learning, that only the learner could write the assignment. Another approach is to actively encourage re-use of existing information by giving marks for the quality of the re-use: the selection, framing and adaptation of the information or ideas. Group assignments are an option as well, even for widely distributed classes. Jointly developed Web pages and online presentations make excellent assignments which develop elearning skills and reinforce the notion that interaction adds value to information.

Technology Literacy

The ability to use computers and other technology to improve learning, productivity, and performance, is a general definition of technology literacy. In fact, openness to new technologies and the willingness to try out new software and new communications opportunities are more important than expertise with a wide range of software.

The point of technology literacy is to prepare students to be morally responsible citizens, actively participating in shaping the nation's technological future, rather than merely reacting to it as passive consumers. All technologies, after all, have social effects and many have had profound moral and political repercussions as well. . . Helping all students prepare to take part in this kind of democratic decision-making is a major new challenge for educators precisely because advanced technologies have become so dominant in our culture. Ultimately, how well our schools and colleges educate students for this kind of thoughtful technological citizenship is far more critical to the future of democracy than how well they train students to operate the latest generation of computers. (The Alliance for Childhood, 1999, p. 2)

Fundamentally this kind of teaching rests on the understanding that the technology is *a* tool, not *the* tool. It is amazing to see the disarray caused when teachers and students are obliged to change platforms. Some annoyance and frustration are understandable when routines are disrupted, but when people feel that the learning resides in the platform rather than the people, it is time for a rethink.

The Connecticon as a Trap

There is no doubt that for each of the positive attributes of the Connecticon, there are equal and opposite dangers. These take many forms: information overload, stress and obsessive behaviours. The seductive and addictive qualities of the Internet have led researchers to carry out studies on students to determine the extent to which connectivity actually hinders concentration on learning. One such study noted:

> Undergraduates expressed concerns about personal control over the ubiquitous and compelling diversions of the Internet, particularly in relationship to productive use of their time. Students described IM [Instant Messaging] as an urgent distraction that required immediate attention regardless of what other activity engaged their attention, implying a negative influence on academic work. Feelings of being out of control during Internet use were frequently expressed. As one female student commented, "I can get sucked in so easily, and will be doing things, and forget the things I have to do online." (Matthews & Schrum, 2003, p. 129)

Another study identified 8% of a 277 undergraduate sample as "pathological Internet users" based on their reports of experiencing greater social ease online than in face-to-face interactions (Morahan-Martin & Schumacher, 2000). Extensive use of synchronous communication systems such as chats and multiuser discussions was associated with impaired academic achievement and social isolation for approximately 9% of undergraduates in one large undergraduate survey (Kubey et al., 2001).

Loss of privacy is another of the worrying aspects of greater connectivity. The more connected I am, the more data about me is known by other systems and other people. Rheingold paints the following picture of the connected future:

In the recent past, it was said that digital information technology, such as the magnetic strips on credit cards, leaves a "trail of electronic breadcrumbs" that can be used to track individuals. In the future, the trail will become a moving cloud as individuals broadcast information about themselves to devices within ten yards, a city block or the entire world. Although there is room for speculation about how quickly the new tools will be adopted, certainly over the next several decades inexpensive wireless devices will penetrate into every part of the social world, bringing efficiencies to the production of snooping power. The surveillance state that Orwell feared was puny in its power in comparison to the panoptic Web we have woven around us. Detailed information about the minute-by-minute behaviours of entire populations will be come cost-effective and increasingly accurate. Both powerfully beneficial and powerfully dangerous potentials of this new tracking capability will be literally embedded in the environment. (Rheingold, 2002, p. xxi)

It is a fascinating phenomenon the way in which increased connectivity is leading to much greater stress for so many people. Courses are now offered in "work/life balance," as an antidote to the overload, overwork and obsession with technology-created connectivity. Given the amount of information stored in even a small library, it might be hypothesised that people should find a library to be a stressful environment. Yet the contrary seems to be the case. The Connecticon, on the other hand, causes most people at times to suffer from overload, stress and even various levels of addiction. Why is this?

The Exponential Growth in Information

The most important characteristic of our present society may well be the incredible speed with which it changes. Whether things evolve in a positive or in a negative way, change itself constitutes a problem. Scientific, techno-logical, cultural and social innovations are taking place at such a breathtak-ing pace that no one can really keep up with them. Yesterday's revolutionary new product has become commonplace today, and will be outdated tomorrow. People constantly need to revise their skills in order to adapt to the changing circumstances. The problems of unemployment and growing disparity between richer and poorer classes in most Western nations are largely due to the fact that not everybody can cope as well with this need for constant reeducation. As traditional agricultural and indus-trial jobs are disappearing, employees need to adapt to the intellectually much more demanding jobs of the information society. Many lack the nec-essary skills and educational background to adapt quickly enough.

Computers have played a large part in the exponential growth of information over the last half century. What has made an even more significant difference in the last fifteen years is the networked computer.

> Curious things happen when you connect all to all. Mathematicians have proven that the sum of a network increases as the square of the number of members. In other words, as the number of nodes in a network increases arithmetically, the value of the network increases exponentially. (Kelly, 1997)

What makes the information of the Connecticon so overwhelming, is the connected nature of the communication. It is many-to-many; it is all pervasive; it is always on. New skills are needed to cope with the quantity and quality of information which surrounds us.

> We cannot continue to apply concepts, laws, practices and the like that were developed to deal with the economic world of goods to the emerging economic world of information. (Lankshear & Knoble, 2001)

Most people are at the mercy of the information, phone calls, email and connected opportunities that bombard them daily. The Web is full of helpful sites, courses and portals on stress management, communication anxiety, and information overload. The problem is recognised, but persists nonetheless. As usual, the social and psychological reactions to the technology have not kept pace with our ability to design and implement innovative uses of it.

A worldwide survey commissioned by Reuters found that two thirds of managers suffer from increased tension and one third from ill-health because of information overload. The psychologist David Lewis, who analysed the findings of this survey (Lewis, 1999) proposed the term "Information Fatigue Syndrome" to describe the resulting symptoms. Other effects of too much information include anxiety, poor decision-making, difficulties in memorizing and remembering, and reduced attention span. These effects merely add to the stress caused by the need to constantly adapt to a changing situation.

Part of the problem is caused by the fact that technological advances have made the retrieval, production and distribution of information so much easier than in earlier periods. This has reduced the natural selection processes which would otherwise have kept all but the most important information from being published. The result is an explosion in often irrelevant, unclear and inaccurate data fragments, making it ever more difficult to see the forest through the trees. This overabundance of low quality information, which Shenk (1997) has called "data smog," is comparable in its emergence and effects to the pollution of rivers and seas caused by an excess of fertilizers, or to the health problems caused by a diet too rich in calories.

The Attention Economy

Unlike information, attention is a scare resource, and with the super-abundance of information we now experience, it is attention which is already the basic currency of the Internet. The experience of information overload is more appropriately understood as an overload of attention-grabbing opportunities.

> We live in an attention economy. At this point in history, capital, labor, and information are all in plentiful supply. Computer processing power increases by leaps and bounds, but the processing power of the human brain stays the same. Telecommunications bandwidth is not a problem; human bandwidth is. (Davenport, 2001)

The advertising world has long known the secrets of attracting and maintaining attention. Educators have rarely seen their role in the same light. Those involved in teaching online, however, are beginning to investigate how elearning is affected by the growing shortage of attention. For example, there is tacit agreement that elearning which is personalised, concise, emotionally evocative and from a trustworthy source, will attract more attention from learners than information without some or all of these characteristics.

Understanding how and where to direct one's attention and capitalising on its value and power are essential skills for living in the Connecticon. Intelligent software agents, specialized bots, data-mining and so on, may be part of the solution, but mastering the economics of attention will demand far more than technical solutions (Lankshear & Knoble, 2001).

Wider Social Changes

The Connecticon may be a powerful force in the world, but it is not the only one. There is a network of interrelated changes of which the Connecticon is but a part. This can be seen forcibly in relation to education and educational institutions, where globalization, commodification of knowledge and marketization are related forces impacting on the change process.

The last ten years have seen increasing challenges to the conventional model of the university, defined in traditional terms by research and liberal education. New providers of higher education are emerging, and increasingly these are privately owned and operating "for profit." Sometimes they use the title "university" (e.g., the UK eUniversities) and often they operate globally with the help of information and communications technologies. Of course many of these new start-ups collapsed after the dot com boom. Nevertheless, the national predominance of long-established universities is seen to be on the decline. There is increasing permeability of borders in higher education, both geographical and conceptual, which results in boundaries which are less strongly delineated than before.

Brokers of educational services are also appearing in the mix of new providers. Established brokers have traditionally operated at regional or national level to offer distance education especially in large countries with dispersed populations (e.g., Canada and Australia). Newer brokerages have begun to act on behalf of institutions, often marketing courses internationally and even commissioning the development of courses which have a known market or client. Finally, some brokers offer services both to institutions (e.g., access to a learning platform, market data, consultancy in how to support online learning) and to learners (e.g., assessment services, technology support). Global University Alliance (GUA) is a consortium of ten universities and Universitas 21st are two examples of global partnerships. Sylvan International is a successful for-profit institution offering tutoring and assessment amongst other provisions. Click2Learn is an example of a provider of online IT materials and NIIT based in India is another. Finally, the three multinational publishers, McGraw-Hill, Pearson and Thomson offer learning materials and a learning platform on which to create content (Garret, 2003).

Larger social and economic trends lie behind this rise of new providers. The growth of knowledge-based economies and the recognition by governments that increased human capital investment is necessary for national competitiveness are two such trends. The individual desire for better employment and social mobility, as well as employees' awareness of the need for lifelong learning and continuous professional development are other factors. Many countries regard the rise of new providers of education and training as the best way of providing additional capacity in reaching the growing pool of potential learners.

A recent World Bank (2002) report on higher education suggests that knowledge is one of the most important motors of economic growth in emerging economies and recommends to governments in developing countries that they keep the regulatory regimes inhibiting virtual and private providers to a minimum. In a climate of increased global competitiveness, particularly over the means for securing economic development and prosperity, universities are seen as key elements and facilitators of the knowledge-based society. That is, rather than investing in physical or financial capital as the best route to economic rewards, investing in people—by enhancing their knowledge, ideas and intellectual abilities—is regarded as more effective. People need to be more skilled and businesses need to be more innovative to meet the competitive challenges of the global economy.

Universities themselves are responding to this competition by becoming more entrepreneurial and "businesslike." Some are taking on the characteristics of the private sector, for-profit bodies, both in their outlook and in their management forms. It is not difficult to draw direct connections between the commodification of knowledge, the rising notion of university education as a business and the utilitarian view of the benefits of higher education. A number of universities, particularly in America, have established for-profit arms to exploit the interest in online learning. Not many of them survived the dot.com crash. Nevertheless, there are doubts about the ability of universities to reform their curricula and research orientations to more explicitly facilitate economic growth and to deliver what employers want. To a large extent this accounts for the rise in private and corporate universities during the 1990s.

The term "disintermediation" has arisen to describe the breakup of educational provision into discreet activities. Instead of the university providing teaching, counselling, examining, accrediting, researching, housing for students and library resources, these components are in some cases being outsourced to different providers. Students can study content provided by a university but be tutored by another, perhaps commercial, provider. They might register for an examination offered by another body. This trend is fiercely denounced by many academics, who regard learning as a holistic process and teaching as an integral process with research.

The effect of globalization on the curriculum has been towards greater internationalisation. Universities are beginning to recognize that much subject content is too domestically oriented in an era when graduates—domestic and international—are facing the prospect of more globally mobile careers. International law, global telecommunications, engineering and business are examples of sectors that require knowledge of international standards and different national cultures and codes for successful employment. The popularity of curriculum areas has changed as well: strong preferences for information technology and business programmes; reduced interest in basic or theoretical research.

We can see that there is a wide range of forces driving change in higher education. The Connecticon is both cause and effect, both driver and vehicle, but certainly not the only or even the major cause of the turmoil and necessity for change.

CONCLUSION

We have introduced the notion of the Connecticon because we are convinced that connectivity has increased to such an extent and in such a way that a new concept is emerging. We do not wish to add to the hype which has so dominated discussion of the Internet. We have tried to convey the dangers as well as the opportunities of the situation. It is by no means an undiluted benefit. Even the benefits have side effects, especially in teaching and learning. Our response to this phenomenon is that we need to learn how to operate within this new context and especially to understand its benefits for learners.

> This emerging new economy represents a tectonic upheaval in our commonwealth, a social shift that reorders our lives more than mere hardware or software ever can. It has its own distinct opportunities and its own new rules. Those who play by the new rules will prosper; those who ignore them will not. (Kelly, 1997)

What we hope to provide is an informed consideration—in the domain of learning—of where hyper-connectivity is leading us and how we should respond.

CHAPTER 2

The Concept of Community

It is critical to our further discussions and analysis that we should agree upon the concept of "community." This is not as easy as it may seem. The difficulty is that "community" appears to mean different things to different groups of people, some of whom even deny that there is such a concept, or that it is a useful way of thinking. As a scientific concept, the idea of community is very broad, with a host of common defining features, which have changed with time and

Source: David Austin and the National Council for Voluntary Organizations.

with relation to different academic disciplines. Business people and economists tend to use it to refer to some aspects of their customer base; natural scientists regard it as an identifiable assemblage of species in a certain habitat; geographers and planners have historically focused on spatial aspects, the characteristics of a physical location, while sociologists emphasize the interactions and networks between members of society. For our purposes, all of these descriptions and none of them hold the full answer.

Yet it is important that we have at least a clear working definition, even if we amend or reject this subsequently. We cannot begin to clarify how online communities actually function, nor compare their successes and

The Connecticon: Learning for the Connected Generation, pages 17–33
Copyright © 2004 by Information Age Publishing

failures to the operations of a physical "on-site" community, if we cannot agree what constitutes such a community, and by definition, what does not. It has been said that "community is one of those many things that we recognize chiefly in their absence," and that "people who break their ties to traditional community are free to live where they want, do what they want, create their own norms and values" (Cobb, p. 1996, p. 185). This is only true to a limited extent, and it does not really explain why humans seek each other out, in groups, clubs, societies, and special interest organizations, gathering together in diverse communities of interest, however informal and/or transient they may be. Though most early work related to the concept of community as a physical territory where residents interact, there was also a contrasting view of community as "an interactional field held together by the human need to interact with other human beings" (Allen, 1993, p. 156). Due to the ability to utilize the Internet to create abstract places (virtual offices, hybrid libraries, online work spaces, and spaces for peer-to-peer interactive games), representations of the self (online identities), and abstract interactions (with other identities and with automated tasks) (Streibel, 1998), it is this latter view of community which has come to be applied to online social networks.

WHAT IS A COMMUNITY?

In an early but influential work, ninety-four definitions of community were classified, using sixteen different concepts. Even this recognized that other definitions were possible and that "When all of the definitions are viewed, beyond the concept that people are involved in community, there is no complete agreement as to the nature of community" (Hillery, 1955, p. 119). Fortunately there were some clear points of convergence around the ideas that community should share either a common geographical area, or that there should be "the presence of some common characteristic other than area." All but three of the definitions stressed social interaction as a necessary element in community life, and if the concept of a shared geographical area is omitted from consideration, then three-quarters of the definitions require a group of people in social interaction having some ties or bonds in common. Hillery suggests that these common characteristics may be such factors as community self-sufficiency, social life, a consciousness of its own kind, or ends, norms, and means to which the community subscribes. In this context he gives two quotations from other authors describing a community as "a social system . . . of interconnected culture bearers." and as "a group of people inhabiting a limited area, who have a sense of belonging together and who through their organized relationships share and carry on activities in pursuit of their common interest" (Hillery, 1955, p. 117)

At the very least then, a community seems to be distinguished by a shared understanding of its boundaries, whether these are geographical, or defined by particular areas of common interest. In passing, Hillery observes that the common bond of sharing a geographical area is a particularly strong definition of community among sociologists studying rural life. He suggests that this association is more easily recognized in rural areas than in urban communities, the latter being larger social units which have a number of secondary groups within the same territory, and a greater heterogeneity of groups. These themes are picked up in an analysis of the importance of locality and community in rural Wales. They draw attention to the fact "that people's location within particular places tended to be an important aspect of their lived experience" (Day & Murdoch, 1993, p. 84), and that "the boundaries between analytically distinct components of life, such as economic relations, cultural understandings, and political goals, may be extremely ill-defined." Their emphasis on locality is primarily spatial or geographical, and they consider the effects of making the local labor market (or travel to work area) the defining characteristic of the locality. They also note that, "labor market boundaries are different for various groups," and that "social relations outside the workplace are not necessarily confined within local labor markets." Drawing upon previous work, they describe "institutional links extending beyond the locality as "vertical" relationships, while those within the locality are "horizontal". This raises interesting possibilities for the concept of overlapping communities of interest and identity within the same geographical locality, and we shall explore this later.

These common activities help to create a sense of community by providing a common sense of identity (Bajan, 1998), with which the members of the community can associate themselves. The work of Day and Murdoch found "a certain stability built around the farm economy, and some interdependencies that connect local services (shops, pubs, petrol station) into this economy" (Day & Murdoch, 1993, p. 95). As a result they concluded that the economic viability of family farming provided a key role in maintaining the structure of social relations. This analysis is echoed by Kemmis (1996) who cites the mutual support given by farming families on the high plains of Montana in activities such as the construction of a new barn, whole families working together despite their very different personal behaviors and lifestyle preferences. This growth of trust between members of a community is an important factor in community success, and those common factors that help shape the behavior of community members become practiced habits that help to construct the norms and identity of the community as a whole. We will explore these key places and core activities a little later, but first it is worth noting another conclusion of Day and Murdoch which extends this sense of identity, namely the awareness of an individual of belonging to a community, and links with the concept of social capital. Though "the district is compact enough, and the population small enough, for it to be possible to know everyone in the vicinity," they found marked differences between the various settlements within the district. One manifestation of this was that one settlement seemed to run clubs and societies very well, and was thought to be "lively," while another was said to be in decline, lacking any real focus, and losing its sense of community. The key point to notice is that the strength of the networks was perceived to impart a heightened vitality, and contributed to the strong sense of community identity in the district. This was developed by Gilchrist (2000) who thought that community is both the outcome and the context of informal networking, with the "well-connected community" being achieved when people feel part of a web of diverse and interlocking relationships.

SOCIAL CAPITAL

There has been much discussion of the concept of social capital, and it is worth trying to summarize the concept here before we go on to investigate evidence for its presence in geographical and online communities. In the 1990s some social scientists began to look at the nature of community in a different way. Cobb (1996, p. 185) made the case that the more strongly people identify themselves by their membership of a community, and the more they feel that they have a full role to play in the life and decision-making roles of their community, then the more strongly that group actually functions as a community. A number of sociological and ethnographical works have scrutinized the detailed interactions of geographical communities, often rural communities, (Allen & Dillman, 1994; Parman, 1990) noting in particular the participation by community members in informal networks and chance individual encounters during which information (and through this, learning) was exchanged. These networks of social interaction are constructed and reinforced through the activities of everyday life and cultural rituals that create interpersonal ties and affirm community boundaries. These types of observations were noted by Portes (1998) who suggested that while economic capital resides in people's bank accounts, and human capital is inside their heads, then social capital is vested in the structure of their relationships. People's sense of community is derived from their perception of being linked into a complex system of relationships and interaction, and these shared experiences help to foster group solidarity and a sense of common purpose (Gilchrist, 2000).

In a seminal article, Putnam (1995) defined social capital as a feature of social organization such as networks, norms, and social trust that facilitate coordination and cooperation for mutual benefit. This connection by people to the life of their community, he termed "civic engagement," and includes membership of local clubs, societies, and associations. By acting together in a common space, members of a community learn from each other to foster a sense of collective identity, which they seek to define and reinforce by constructing "rules" of behavior (however rigid or loose) through which they can achieve a general consensus that is consistent with their common interests. The ways by which these norms are constructed, reinforced, and enforced will be different between different communities, and this is as true between geographical communities as it is between geographical and "virtual" communities. In this context it has been suggested that:

> the well-connected community has strong internal relationships, but also valuable and challenging links with people and organisations beyond its own membership and immediate vicinity. It may have a strong collective identity... but its defining edges are fuzzy. (Gilchrist, 2000, p. 269)

In studying the evolution of online communities Preece (2002) noted two challenges, the first is to focus on developing technologies that are accessible to a wide range of users on a variety of devices. The second is to ensure that the software supports effective social interaction online. In communities of place and online communities, it is important to understand that:

> networking is a vital component of community development practice because it creates the conditions for robust, yet flexible forms of collective action. (Gilchrist, 2000)

A key community-building element resulting from social networking is the fostering of trust between the members of the network, partly from sharing stories and partly through being exposed to the stories of participants who seem to be similar to themselves in some ways, but to be different in other ways. The Web has emerged as a new technological vehicle for harvesting the personal experiences of others (Glogoff, 2001) and the construction of tools that attempt to make this collective activity more visible (and accessible) is a major research field (Erickson et al., 2002).

It is clear from numerous studies (Blanchard & Horan, 1998; Rheingold, 2000) that reciprocal support is a vital part of community networks, both online and in a physical location, though this may manifest itself in a wide range of support, from baby-sitting, to practical comfort in times of stress, to the praise and celebration of a successful task well done. At the heart of collaborative activity, there is an understanding that participants contribute something positive when they are able to, in the realization that they may be required to draw on the support of others at some point in the future. Social capital, sometimes referred to as "the glue that holds a community together" increases a community's productive potential in several ways, "it promotes business networking, shared leads, equipment and services, joint ventures, faster information flows and more agile transactions"(Wilson, 1997, p. 3). The right to participate in community decision-making brings the responsibility to act for the common good, and in the realization that social capital is essential for maintaining and enhancing the value of public goods, Dhesi has noted that:

> most forms of social capital come into being through the combined actions of several or many people. The decisions of each has consequences for all. So it is an attitude of social structures. It is not the private property of any one person who benefits from it all. It exists only when it is shared. (Dhesi, 2000, p. 3)

This is an important aspect of collaborative learning activities, and the many-to-many accessibility of online interactive networks means that "virtual communities" have profound implications not simply for learning, but for understanding social change in general.

VIRTUAL COMMUNITIES

The term "virtual communities" has increasingly been applied to communication networks in which the participants are not located in the same geographical place, but are distributed across the globe. Unfortunately the term seems to have almost as many definitions and descriptions as the "traditional" communities of place, and almost as many detractors. Ehrenfeld (1996) dismissed assemblages of electronically linked people as "pseudocommunities," and took a negative perspective of their contribution to contemporary society in the United States. Although his assertion that, "the passions and activities of love, hatred, sexuality, compassion, selfishness, and intellectual intercourse, modulated by and expressed through the life of the community, take on a complexity and richness that are not found in an electronically facilitated pseudocommunity," may seem rather dated already, and would be hotly contested by many practitioners (e.g., Blanchard & Horan, 1998; Wellman & Gulia, 1999) he has a more serious dissent. As with other critics of the social value of online communities, he maintains that online communication, such as e-mail, creates the sensation of being part of a community of people, interacting for the common good, but is substantially an illusion (Ehrenfeld, 1996). This is difficult to counter, for two main reasons, first the complex and diverse interactions that take place in "real" communities of place are not fully understood and many are contested by academics (e.g., we don't appear to regard our regular network of telephone contacts, or our superficial but regular contacts made through our work as anything other than real communities.) Second, the scope and depth of online contacts are so wide, from the occasional e-mail inquiry from a friend-of-a-friend, to active many-to-many academic discussion lists, to the detailed collaborative information sharing on groove networks, or other shared work spaces, that it seems foolish and irresponsible to catalogue all online relationships as illusory or superficial. While it is true that electronic communications (phone, video-conferences, e-mail, and shared desktops) create the illusion of proximity between participants, our question is whether proximity is a mandatory requirement for a community, or whether in this instance, the liberating results of technology have allowed us to ameliorate, if not remove, the tyranny of distance.

In our experience, and as we shall try to document later in this book, there are many similarities between geographical communities and online communities in their function and in the process of their operation. While it is true that there are very many differences between geographical and online communities, there are also many differences within the form and function of geographical communities of place. The key function, as we will see, lies in the opportunities for interaction between members of the community, particularly with regard to the maintenance of dialogue and the promotion of conversation. Shared conversations lead to greater collaboration, the spread of reciprocal benefits, and the fostering of a communal sense of identity is based upon shared interest and mutual trust.

In attempting to define normative community, Cobb (1996, p. 185) notes three key characteristics: the mutual responsibility which members of the community share, the role of the community in defining the identity of its members, and the degree to which members must participate in the life and decisions of the community. Although he was primarily talking about "real" communities, it was significant that he noted that, "not all communities, considered as givers of personal identity, are geographical" and that "the breakdown of traditional communities has made self-identification in non-geographical ways increasingly important." He gave the Jewish Diaspora and the worldwide community of scientists as examples of "non-geographical groups identified as accepting mutual responsibility within the group," and drew attention to the fact that "multiple types of self-identification play major roles in different aspects of an individual's life." Other studies have focused upon communities of common-interest groups, such as General (medical) Practitioners to compare similarities and discrepancies between online and face-to-face interactions (Fox & Roberts, 1999). This ability for different aspects of the human personality and individual values to assume different levels of priority in diverse groups of people (communities) is an important driving factor in the growth of online communities.

Simply because an online community has a less tangible physical presence (because the community is dispersed and may never meet face-to-face) does not negate its existence. A useful comparison might be made with our references to the political "sphere of influence" which makes recognition of subtle civic and political communications and allegiances, only some, or none of which, may operate through a face-to-face network of players. Similarly the social construction made by economists called "the market" to describe the local or global interplay of economic processes involving supply and demand is not weakened because there is no physical marketplace where all the participants can sit down face-to-face to negotiate their complex deals. The invention of the "virtual community" as a term to describe computer networked interactions is not consistent if it is not also applied to earlier forms of distributed interactive networks. It was a useful term to give a shorthand description of the exciting and rapid appearance of a wider range of global connections through computer mediated communications, but on closer analysis, with more persistent usage, the term has become an overused, redundant, and misleading appellation.

For this and a number of other reasons we would suggest that it is not helpful to continue to refer to the collective operation of groups of people who communicate socially and professionally through electronic media as "virtual communities." We would prefer to describe them as "online interactive networks', and refer to them as "Connecticon spaces" where people meet online, in the sense that an increasing number of scientific analyses indicate that the members of these communities frequently feel that the interaction they have with their online colleagues is closer than the human relationships that they have with their near neighbors or workmates who happen to be close to their geographical location (Blanchard & Horan, 1998; Rheingold, 2000).

TYPES OF ONLINE INTERACTIVE NETWORKS

Blanchard and Horan (1998) identified two types of online communities (Connecticon spaces) which they termed physically based virtual community and second, virtual communities of interest. In the first type a geographical locality—village, town, or city—develops electronic resources for its citizens, enabling them to interact and share information in a wider variety of ways. In the second type the community is normally geographically dispersed, with members participating due to their shared interest in a topic, not because of their shared geographical location. More generally, we might refer to them in the language of Falk and Kirkpatrick who proposed the term "communities of common purpose" to describe:

> this kind of contemporary community of people, noting as we do that people may have multiple memberships of such communities-of-common-purpose, and that the life of the communities tends to be variable and defined by its purpose. (Falk & Kilpatrick, 2000, p. 103)

In an increasingly electronically networked world we may occupy both of these communities at different times of our day, working, learning, and socializing. Online groups have the ability to connect with their community of interest at any time of day or night to share information or solicit help, and it is common that online relationships also move to include other forms of communication (e.g., telephone, post and/or face-to-face interaction).

The classification of online communities was taken further (Marathe, 1999) by a consideration of four principle types based upon the primary motivation of the participants. These can be considered as:

1. **Communities of purpose**, formed by people who are trying to achieve a similar objective, who assist each other by sharing experiences, information, and peer-to-peer knowledge.
2. **Communities of practice**, formed by groups of people sharing a similar profession or vocation who seek to share experiences and facilitate professional exchange (which may also add value to offline networks)
3. **Communities of circumstance**, which are similar to communities of practice but are generally more personally focused, or related to life experiences, and not driven by professional activities.
4. **Communities of interest**, linking people who share their ideas, passion, and knowledge in a common interest or theme, but might know very little about each other outside this shared interest.

To this we would tentatively add a fifth classification,

5. **Communities of users**, who are represented by the more innovative and interactive business networks that allow customer to customer exchanges, including the sharing of information, reviews, and specific themed discussions.

These communities, and hybrid variations will be discussed later in this book, but for the moment it is useful to consider some of the key characteristics that define online interactive networks. Later we will become more particularly focused on online *learning* communities, for of course not all community activities offer the same opportunities for learning, and consequently the structures and criteria for successful community life will vary.

KEY ACTIVITIES OF AN ONLINE INTERACTIVE NETWORK

It seems reasonable to agree that a community provides a framework of shared beliefs, interests, and commitments that unite a set of varied individuals, groups, and activities. Some of these shared factors are central, others more peripheral, "but all are connected by bonds that establish a common faith, a personal identity, a sense of belonging, and a supportive structure of activities and relationships (Selznick, 1996). Common components would seem to be a shared motivation and commitment toward group interaction and a joint responsibility for sharing this interaction. Like its counterpart in communities of place, the level of engagement by individuals in these shared values will vary widely, from the bystanders at a public meeting (lurkers) to activists (online and offline), for some of whom the online experience is simply a way of augmenting their experiences of life. Critics point out the dangers that the "virtual" experience tends to skew the real work, first by making artificial experiences seem real, second by "smoothing" them and making them more compelling than the real, and third by creating the illusion that because they are so "lifelike" that we have actually achieved more than we have in the real experience (Turkle, 1996).

Marathe (1999) listed three key criteria that define successful online communities:

1. **Self-generated evolution**, where members of the community generate the content for the site, and take decisions to influence its growth, adaptation, and evolution.
2. **Involvement and interactivity**, through which members participate and interact with other members of the community (e.g., through e-mail, bulletin boards, synchronous chat etc.)
3. **Frequency and duration of visits**, that encourage members to come back to the site repeatedly in order to share their motivations with other community members as part of the process of establishing a collective identity and sense of trust between members of the community.

There is a clear indication that the participants in online communities are not attracted to them by the provision of tools alone, but need to be able to recognize a common bond with other members of that community.

It is this shared set of experiences which provides the potent stimulant of learning opportunities.

It is too easy to become dogmatic or deterministic in the comparison of communities, whether of place or of common purpose. Selznick (1996) described seven common bonds of a unidimensional community with multiple values:

1. **Historicity**—strands of shared history and culture.
2. **Identity**—a loyalty and sense of belonging to their perception of the community.
3. **Mutuality**—a supportive experience of interdependence and reciprocity.
4. **Plurality**—created by the vitality of intermediate associations, such as families and common interest groups.
5. **Autonomy**—the need to respect the rights of the individual within the community who contributes different views.
6. **Participation**—in the social interconnections of the life of the community.
7. **Integration**—of all the above elements with enough coherence to provide the basis for a common life and understanding of their community.

According to this, the true function of a community is to provide an agreed regulation, discipline, and a conduit for self-expression that is consistent with the greater good of the participant group as a whole. A key mechanism for achieving this is through fostering social institutions, which extends the concept of community beyond clusters of like-minded enthusiasts in common interest groups, to networks of distinct but independent institutions (Selznick, 1996). These heterogeneous networks differentiate the framework of a community from its constituent, narrower, common interest groups.

Nevertheless, it is in these groups that we need to focus to understand the nature of adult learning. Mayes (2002) noted that "The term, lifelong learning, must—if it is to mean anything—convey the importance of an attitude to learning. Attitudes are rooted in the social and cultural environment." He goes on to say that "It is likely that greater insight into pedagogic innovation is to be gained through focusing on the social dimensions of communities of learners than on continuing to view the learner's key relationships as being with the subject matter, or at best with a tutor." In this article, Mayes argues the case that the way in which individual learners identify with particular communities will determine the most fundamental way they think and feel about learning, and as a result "All learning is situated in a personal, social and organizational context, which determines motivation" (Mayes, 2002). In studies relating to the formation of co-operative relationships online, the awareness of other participants' histories and relationships have been observed to be a key factor that is critical in securing a co-operative outcome (Smith, 2002). This will come as no surprise to community development workers and sociologists of rural community networks who will be well aware of the importance of the informal local grapevine that is influenced not just by what you know, but also whom you know. As a direct result, "while information-oriented applications of Internet technology are useful, the more exciting potential of this new learning medium is not about information, but about community and collaboration"(Bruckman, 2002).

This "situated learning" among social and personal experience is well known to those who work in supporting development among geographical communities of space. Numerous studies (e.g., Allen & Dillman, 1994; Oldenburg, 1995)) have analyzed the role of informal public spaces as locations in which people meet, converse, join with friends, and are exposed to chance acquaintances. Conversation is the primary activity in these common areas of public space, the cafes, bars, post offices, village shops, which Oldenburg (1995) termed "third places" (ranked after the home and the workplace) and which he described as the "strollways of the casual environment." In these third places, individuals can relax on neutral ground, meet with friends who share common interests, and encounter chance meetings with people who share different values, some of whom they would not normally socialize within their home or work environment. Third places facilitate easy association and a discovery of different facets of life that add new experiences. When these experiences are shared with a network of friends, it tends to lead to a certain level of trust, mutual tolerance (perhaps understanding) and a shared sense of identity as a group who have "been through things together."

THE CONVERGENCE OF PLACE AND PURPOSE

Although we can consider both communities of place, and communities of shared activity and/or shared belief, there is crucial synergy that develops when a community of purpose is largely located within a single community of place. Numerous studies have observed that new public spaces are created, and opportunities for interaction among members are increased by linking "virtual" communities of interest to physical communities, in campus-based education, telecentres, the extension of business networks, or mail order shopping with like-minded consumers. Key places are sites of interaction that have the potential to build social capital, and as sites of learning, for individuals, businesses, and the local community as a whole. In view of the vast volume of literature studying online communities and their participants, it is surprising that more has not been done to look at the comparisons of online networks that overlap (or interlink) with physical communities of place. We will pick this theme up again in Chapter 5 because:

> to properly understand how virtual communities affect physical communities and the people within them, we must examine virtual communities of interest within physical communities. (Blanchard & Horan, 1998, p. 305)

Many of these attributes of common spaces are shared in the online environment, and though the identification of "third places" may be more difficult to discern, there are strong similarities in the construction, recognition, and reinforcement of these interactive networks. The study of communities of practice, interactive networks based upon a common disciplinary background, with similar work activities, values, tools, and shared stories has indicated five major community themes (Millen, Fontaine, & Muller, 2002) namely:

- **Development path**—how does the community form and evolve?
- **Membership**—how and why do members join, leave, and participate?
- **Activities**—What do members do in the community? How do they interact?
- **Organizational support**—How is the community supported by the organization?
- **Value**—What value do the members receive? How does the organization benefit from the community?

It is significant, in the context of relating the design of online communities to the participant profile that they hope to attract that "Community is no longer defined as a physical place, but as a set of relationships where people interact socially for mutual benefit. Online community is a social network that uses computer support as the basis of communication among members instead of face-to-face interaction" (Andrews, 2002). Two crucial aspects in the development of interactive learning networks, whether online or on-site, are the swift establishment of trust between the participants, and the development of collaborative learning activities (Hiltz & Turoff, 2002). These collaborative activities may include small groups of students reading material on different topics and preparing summaries for the rest of the class, as well as debates, group projects, role-play, and collaborative essays, case studies, or research plans. A key feature to recognize is that in the development of this type of interactive network, the community of learners, becomes the learning network, as much as the computer-based communications system that supports it. To echo our earlier words, the Connecticon comprises the network infrastructure, the human resource that uses it, and the products of the hyper-interactivity between these users that the network can support.

In an attempt to synthesize the lessons of this chapter it is useful to consider the model constructed by Gongla and Rizzuto (2001) to describe the evolution of online communities of practice, defined as "a group of people informally bound together by shared expertise and passion for a joint enterprise." They make a crucial distinction, with which we would agree that "to form a community, it is not sufficient to have individuals who may be doing the same job or existing in the same organizational unit. In order to connect as a community, individuals need to establish personal connections with each other." This is a key feature of interactivity, which helps to establish network norms, rules, trust, and group identity. In this model (summarized in Table 2.1) the authors propose a modification of earlier life-cycle models (McDermott, 2000; Wenger, 1998) and identify a five-stage pattern in the evolution of communities, including potential, building, engaged, active, and adaptive. As communities progress through each stage, they increase their capabilities, though progression is not inevitable, and communities can mature or dissolve at any stage.

Falk and Kilpatrick (2000, p. 89) noted that "any notion of learning presupposes interactions between the social actors themselves and the contextual tools they employ." They observe that the locations of these interactions have a powerful potential to produce "changes in attitudes, skills, knowledge and behavior. It is therefore the point at which learning may be seen to occur." In their analysis of communities of practice as applied to the business context, Gongla and Rizzuto (2001) were at pains to point out that each community they observed had its unique personality, strengths and challenges, and in that communities in their evolutionary model could move back and forth between stages. This is an important point, for it recognizes that every community has the potential to contribute positively to its wider social environment, and through this process to influence and reflect change. In particular, their assertion that:

> even communities that are in a continual stage of building can provide a magnet for capturing and sharing intellectual capital and attracting skilled resources. (Gongla & Rizzuto, 2001, p. 859)

This has profound implications for how we structure online learning, and how we manage the learning environment, so we should now take a look at these aspects in more depth.

Table 2.1. The Evolution of Communities of Practice (Gongla & Rizzuto, 2001)

	Potential	Building	Engaged	Active	Adaptive
Definition	A community is forming	The community defines itself and formalises its operating principles.	The community executes and improves its processes.	The community understands and demonstrates benefits from knowledge management and the collective work of the community	The community and its supporting organization(s) are using knowledge for competitive advantage
Fundamental Functions	Connection	Memory and context creation	Access and learning	Collaboration	Innovation and generation
People Behavior	Individuals find one another and link up. The organization may be unaware of or uninterested in the potential community OR The organization may provide some support to locate and introduce individuals.	Core Members: • Learn about each other. • Share experiences and knowledge. • Build common vocabulary. • Create roles and norms. • Begin a formal history together and record it. • Start a repertoire of stories. The organization recognises the community.	Members: • Develop trust in and loyalty to the community. • Commit to the community. • Outreach to new members. • Model technology-sharing behaviour. • Tell community stories. • Actively search for and contribute material to build the community knowledge base. • Promote and participate in knowledge sharing. The organisation interacts with the community and learns of its capabilities.	Individuals engage other community members to solve problems and do "real work." The community creates focussed work groups. The community connects to and interacts with other communities. The organization actively supports and measures community work. The organization begins to rely on the community's knowledge to contribute to business value.	The community changes its environment through creation of new products, new markets, new businesses. Members working together advance the knowledge, and even the definition, of their field. The community sponsors new communities. The organization uses the community to develop new capabilities and to respond to and influence markets.

Table 2.1. The Evolution of Communities of Practice (Gongla & Rizzuto, 2001) (Cont.)

	Potential	Building	Engaged	Active	Adaptive
Process Support	Identifying potential community members. Locating potential community members. Facilitating bringing individuals together.	Classifying and storing knowledge. Developing ways to support the knowledge life cycle. Planning for community operation. Beginning deployment.	Socialising new members. Managing workflow. Executing life-cycle process for developing and managing knowledge. Supporting tacit knowledge exchange. Developing and disseminating communications. Gathering and managing feedback. Correcting problems and adjusting. Re-examining and modifying community definition and scope. Ensuring self-governance and self-regulation.	Problem-solving and decision-making. Sensing and assessing the organisational environment. Enhancing the community learning and feedback processes. Integrating with organizational processes. Linking with other communities.	Adapting responsively to the environment, exhibiting dynamic stability. Developing advanced boundary processes. Mentoring the formation of new communities. Focussing on innovation.
Enabling Technology	Electronic messaging systems: e-mail, chat rooms, lists. Phone calls and teleconferences. On-line forums. On-line directories.	Common repository. Initial classification and categorization schema tools. Document and library management systems. Collaborative work environment.	Portals. Expert and community "yellow pages" or locators. Language translation capabilities. Electronic surveys, polling, and other community-sensing or feedback tools.	Electronic meetings. Collaboration tools, such as for issue-based discussion. Team work rooms. Analytical and decision-making tools. Integration of community technology with the applications & technology of the organisation.	Pilot uses of technology. Integration with the technologies of external organizations. Technology transfer.

SUMMARY

In this chapter we have:

- Suggested that the concept of community should be regarded as a network of individuals who share common interests and/or a common set of values, and whose members engage in the exchange of personal connections.
- Proposed that the term "virtual communities" to describe online interactive networks should be discontinued in favor of the concept of "Connecticon spaces." This in view of the observed fact that many participants claim to have just as many close (multiple) connections with their online colleagues as they have with their neighbors in the physical location.
- Agreed that the principle of encouraging full and meaningful collaboration between learners and the stimulation of peer-to-peer interaction are key components of situated learning, which can reap substantial benefits through the incorporation of online activities.
- Indicated that there is a fundamental need for researchers to identify key places that facilitate and stimulate the exchange of experiences, information and learning online (formal and non-formal) that are equivalent to the "third places" existing in physical communities of place.
- Identified that an evolutionary model for the development of interactive online networks has strong potential to assist us in understanding the dynamics of the ways in which online learning and peer-to-peer learning can be analyzed.

CHAPTER 3

Connected Learning

INTRODUCTION

There seems to be little doubt that connectivity is increasingly defining the personal and social landscape. If so, what are the implications for education? Can it be said that connectivity increases learning? Many assume that it does and think that providing

FIRST THE GOOD NEWS, I'M GOING TO DO A DEGREE NOW THE BAD NEWS, I'M NOT LEAVING HOME

ONLINE LEARNING

Source: Robert Thompson, *The Guardian.*

schools with the hardware and software to access the Internet is almost automatically going to improve learning. Governments and funders are continually calling for evidence of increased learning with ICT—and being surprised and frustrated by the lack of solid evidence. Does connectivity increase either the quantity or the quality of learning? Or is this perhaps the wrong question? If connectivity is so pervasive in the workplace and in the "social space," surely education is obliged to reflect this and to prepare

The Connecticon: Learning for the Connected Generation, pages 35–48
Copyright © 2004 by Information Age Publishing

students for the world as it is. Looking for increased learning might be the same fools' gold as looking for cost savings with online learning. If connectivity is the *modus vivendi*, surely "unconnected learning" belongs with the quill pen and the slate board.

In this chapter we will address these questions by analyzing existing research and reflecting on our own experience as online teachers, learners and researchers. First of all, we will begin with a review of learning outcomes from traditional forms of campus-based teaching.

WHAT DO WE KNOW ABOUT FACE-TO-FACE LEARNING?

Take two piano teachers. One is very well trained and gives well-planned lessons in which the pupils progress well. They like the teacher and learn to play with some facility. The other teacher is a real musician, too knowledgeable perhaps and too demanding, but pupils of this teacher really develop a love of music that comes from a deep connection with the piano that the teacher conveys.

In higher education, even in abstract subjects, there are surface approaches and deeper approaches to learning. The extensive educational psychology research—primarily carried out in the United States—that measures student performance on final exams as the outcome criterion, tells us little about the development of deep understanding, and quite a lot about how to produce surface approaches to learning (Morgan, 1993). We need to look at other kinds of research to assess the nature of learning in conventional forms of higher education.

One of the important findings from cognitive psychology reveals the tenacity of prior beliefs and mental models, and their imperviousness to contrary data. For example, Marchese (1997) notes that we all carry in our heads naïve, commonsensical ideas about mechanics that are pre-Newtonian. Wrong as they may be, these views turn out to be ever so resistant to change by conventional instruction...notwithstanding all the right answers we can produce for exams on the subject. However, Hake's (1998) study of physics students shows that more active forms of learning, problem-based labs, and immediate feedback through discussion with peers and/or instructors make a striking difference. Mental models remain difficult to alter, but the nature of the learning environment matters. Active engagement with concepts, and opportunities for informal discussion about them are known to be important elements in a successful learning environment.

Another factor that has been well documented in research is that of learner motivation. In psychological terms, motivation is the process that arouses, sustains and regulates human behavior. Researchers in motivation for learning make a distinction between intrinsic motivation—the growth and striving from within through interest, curiosity or drive for its own sake, and extrinsic motivation which includes such external causes as social approval or disapproval, rewards, promotion or avoiding negative consequences. On the whole, intrinsic motivation is seen to be more lasting and more stable, though extrinsic motivators are still an important part of the mix (Morgan, 1993). However, certain extrinsic motivators can undermine intrinsic curiosity and drive to learn. For example, imposed goals and time lines, surveillance, lack of feedback and an overloaded curriculum can all inhibit intrinsic motivation. By contrast, non-pressuring tactics which give the learner control and choice in what, where and how to learn, are known to be more effective (Martocchio, 1992). External sticks and carrots often appear to be effective in the short term, but rarely sustain the complex task of deep level understanding. There are worrying signs that this lesson has not been learned by software developers:

> Overbearing tracking of users during the learning process could be counter-productive. A Learning Management System that explicitly makes the learner aware that every detail is being recorded could undermine the very idea of a learning culture. This has some serious implications for the elearning industry, which has wedded itself to a command and control structure of surveillance through software tracking. (Clark, 2003a, p. 10)

Self confidence and self-awareness as a learner are significant factors for persistence in learning, in overcoming difficulties and seeking help. Learning opportunities that develop the individual's confidence and deepen understanding of personal learning styles are known to be more effective than a "one size fits all" approach to teaching. For example, Boud (1995) has carried out extensive research in the area of assessment and has shown the debilitating results on students—sometimes causing a lifetime's antipathy to formal education—from procedures that undermine students' self-confidence as learners.

Motivation is not a single quality cast in concrete for each individual learner. It changes over time as internal drive fluctuates and external factors impinge on the learner. It is clear from surveys that many people have been de-motivated by their learning experiences whether at school, higher education or the workplace (National Adult Learning, 2001). What is interesting is that so many people learn in spite of teaching situations that fall so short of the ideal. The concern is that, as we enter a world in which knowledge and know-how are more central than ever before, we can no longer afford to rely on "learning in spite of bad teaching."

These two issues—active learning and motivation—are actually common sense observations that have been confirmed through research about how to make learning effective. A report by Ewell (1997) lists a number of other things we know about learning (but usually fail to implement in traditional campus-based higher education):

- The learner is not a "receptacle" of knowledge, but rather creates his or her learning actively and uniquely.
- Learners constantly rework patterns, relationships and connections using different learning styles that need to be accommodated in instructional models.
- Formal learning situations are only a small part of the learning experience—most learning happens implicitly.
- Direct experience decisively shapes individual understanding.
- Learning occurs best in the context of a compelling "presenting problem," i.e., one that is challenging but not overwhelming.
- Beyond stimulation, learning requires reflection in order to build lasting cognitive connections.
- Learning occurs best in a cultural context that provides both enjoyable interaction and substantial personal support (adapted from Ewell, 1997).

As Ewell points out, "Taken individually, each of these insights about the nature of learning isn't much of a surprise. But colleges and universities remain 'novice cultures' in developing approaches consistent with these 'obvious' insights" (Ewell, 1997, p. 2).

It is not difficult to construct from this list, an outline of what constitutes an effective learning environment: one that emphasizes application of ideas and active experiences, interpersonal collaboration, and feedback on performance. Teachers themselves need to act as models of the learning process, and offer opportunities for learners to make connections and develop cross-disciplinary skills. It is clear from this list that face-to-face teaching could address all of these learning requirements, and as we will demonstrate in later chapters, so can online learning. The issue is not whether one medium is better than another; it is about creating an effective learning environment whatever the medium. However, there are wider social, economic and political considerations that impinge on the methods and medium appropriate for higher education at any point in time.

WHY TRADITIONAL TEACHING NEEDS TO CHANGE

The essential message of this book is that the content and the processes of most current education need to change—because of the impact of connectivity on society in general and therefore on the skills, attitudes and understandings needed by tomorrow's students. The changes required are not revolutionary so much as evolutionary. They derive partly from the growing understanding that knowledge is socially constructed rather than discovered. "We construct and maintain knowledge, not by examining the world but by negotiating with one another in communities of knowledgeable peers" (Bruffee, 1993, p. 9). "Knowledge is therefore not universal and absolute. It is local and historically changing. We construct and reconstruct it, time after time, and build it up in layers" (Bruffee, 1993, p. 222).

This same thinking about the origin of knowledge has emerged from the workplace as well. In the *Fifth Discipline*, Peter Senge (1990) discusses the emergence of new knowledge through dialogue with peers. He advocates a "shift of mind—from seeing ourselves as separate from the world to connected to the world, from seeing problems as caused by someone or something 'out there' to seeing how our own actions create the problems we experience. A learning organization is a place where people are continually discovering how they create their reality. And how they can change it" (Senge, 1990, pp. 12–13).

The urgency for change has been created by the increase in connectivity, the impact of the Internet and the globalization of economic interaction. We can no longer afford to tolerate rote learning, surface level approaches to learning, examinations that test memorization, lecturers teaching the same material as they did twenty years ago, programs that emphasize quantity over quality of learning, graduates with little understanding of how to carrying on learning throughout the rest of their lives. Ramsden (1992) concludes his analysis of traditional higher education methods thus:

> The reader will now I hope be able to see one step ahead in the argument and confront the inevitable truth that many popular methods, such as the traditional lecture-tutorial-discussion-laboratory-class method of teaching science and social science courses, do not emerge from this analytical process unscathed. In fact, not to put too fine a point on it, many teaching methods in higher education would seem, in terms of our theory, to be actually detrimental to the quality of student learning. (Ramsden, 1992, p. 152)

There are too many other critical skills, perspectives and approaches students need to develop. Some of this knowledge is tacit—like watching an IT expert tackle a computer problem or connectivity breakdown—it is an intricate combination of generic skills, confidence, openness, experience and perseverance that eventually produce the way forward. This is not to imply a philistine agenda for higher education—one in which the purpose of the university is to teach skills that are relevant to the economic prosperity of the nation. Rather, what we advocate is a curriculum, a pedagogy and a learning environment that reflect the prevailing knowledge, context and conditions, and even more, anticipate future developments. The Internet and associated connectivity has already had a profound impact on knowledge, on the context of learning as well as on social conditions generally. In short, what it is to know things, is changing. Lankshear identifies four dimensions of change:

- Changes in "the world (objects, phenomena) to be known" associated with the impact of digitization;
- Changes in conceptions of knowledge and processes of "coming to know";
- Changes in the constitution of "knowers" which reflect the impact of intensified digitization;
- Changes in the relative significance of, and balance among, different modes of knowing associated with digitization (Lankshear, 2003, pp. 167–168).

Theoretically, face-to-face teaching blended with some online connectivity could meet the pedagogical demands of constructivist thinking, deep approaches to learning, revised curricula and student-centered learning. And to some extent, this is the direction higher education institutions are taking. However, there are wider considerations:

- The need to broaden access to higher education. Most countries in the world need a massive increase in the absolute numbers of people going to university. Yet most conventional universities continue to base their reputation on exclusiveness and restricted size.
- For all the group work and collaborative activity that have entered classrooms in recent times, knowledge is seen in the final analysis as a private possession, and is examined and accredited accordingly (Larkshear, 2003).
- The reductions in government funding of higher education experienced by most universities worldwide, leading to a growth of partnering, resource sharing, virtual universities, and globally offered courses.
- The political imperative to reduce the digital divide and to create educational opportunities for developing countries.
- Technological developments creating opportunities for access to vast quantities of information and for connectivity to instructors and other learners.
- The need for learning throughout life—professional updating, career change, just-in-time learning.

These imperatives simply cannot be met by carrying on with traditional forms of teaching and learning or even on-campus blended learning.

IS ELEARNING THE ANSWER?

Elearning is referred to by academics, journalists and researchers as if it were one identifiable type of teaching medium. Of course, the reality is very different, and there is considerable ambiguity and often contradictory conceptions about what constitutes elearning. This is particularly true in the training and workplace use of the term, where some definitions of elearning carry strong overtones of computer-based training transferred to the Internet. The emphasis is on the electronic nature of the content, not the communicative potential of the Web. Practitioners who emphasize the content delivery side of elearning often have a behaviorist or cognitive conception of learning, whether consciously or not. They focus on the development of clearly presented content, facilities for testing the learner and multimedia materials for increasing learner motivation. Access to training, reduced costs, and speed and retention of learning are the attractions of elearning for them.

In the higher education literature, there is greater consensus that online learning or elearning means electronic access and interaction with learning materials, fellow learners and tutors. The focus here is on the communicative potential of elearning, rather than content delivery. Researchers of elearning who emphasize the communicative nature of elearning draw on constructivist and social practice theories of learning, often overtly aiming to transform the role of the instructor to that of a facilitator of knowledge construction, and to create a social environment in which learners learn from each other online. In practice, however, too many elearning courses consist of print-based materials transferred directly to the web, and many elearning components of campus-based courses consist of lecturers' PowerPoint slides available electronically. As with face-to-face learning in higher education, practice in online teaching falls considerably short of both the potential and the documented research on learning.

A recent review of 100 research papers about elearning in higher education identified four major features of good practice (Coomey & Stephenson, 2001):

- *Dialogue:* using email, bulletin boards, "real-time" chat, asynchronous chat, group discussions and debate, the tutor or moderator structure interactive opportunities into the content of the course.
- *Involvement:* includes responses in structured tasks, active engagement with material, collaboration and small group activities.
- *Support:* includes periodic face-to-face contact, online tutorial supervision, peer support, advice from experts, feedback on performance, support services and software tools. Support is the most important

feature of successful online courses, as reported in nearly all of the 100 papers surveyed.

- *Control:* refers to the extent to which learners have control of key learning activities and are encouraged to exercise that control. Responses to exercises, pace and timing, choice of content, management of learning activities, navigation through course content, overall direction and assessment of performance.

This categorization encapsulates well the experiences of the "early adopters" (both students and teachers) of elearning. It is easy to see that the results are in line with research on learning: the importance of interaction and engagement, of feedback and support, and of student-centered learning processes.

As the technology of online learning has improved, however, more innovative approaches have begun to emerge. The leading edge online courses are beginning to exploit the uniqueness of the medium and to move well beyond the thinking that sees face-to-face teaching as the ideal to be copied by other media. Three areas are highlighted here:

1. *The break down of the distinction between teacher and taught.* The web enables students to engage in activities which were previously the domain of the teacher: students can contribute resources to the course content, teach other students through presentations and online seminars, and publish their findings, their assignments and their reports in web resources and weblogs. Peer evaluation is enabled by web-based tools such as shared workspaces. Multimedia assignments with video clips, photos, and web spaces bring a new kind of ownership to student work. Many students have their own website and make links to it in their course activities. Descriptions and evaluations of programs are beginning to appear in the literature where these kinds of student-centered approaches to elearning are resulting in a new form of learning environment (see, e.g., Adelsberger et al., 2002; Segrave & Holt, 2003).

The role of the instructor in leading-edge courses is changing in line with that of the students. Knowledge used to be something acquired through experience over time. Experts were people who knew a lot about a particular subject. With the explosion of information and readily available information, both of these traditional forms of knowledge or expertise are no longer as valid. In the connected world, experts are people who know where to find information, how to make sense of it and what to do with it. Instructors have become facilitators of learning, certainly, but more than that, they need to develop a much broader understanding of the domain in which they teach. Some academics view this new role disparagingly as a waste of their expertise and a loss of power and prestige. In fact, the opposite is really the case. To know what is worth knowing in a field, and to be able to discriminate amongst the vast amount of information which proliferates in most fields, and to model these processes for students, are much more profound attributes than the ability to deliver lectures!

> Educators will spend less time dispensing information and more time receiving, adding value, and redirecting information to where it can do the most good or where it is needed. This will be a cultural shift of massive proportions. (Szabo, 2002, p. 390)

2. *Design for the web.*   Instructional designers are beginning to make effective use of a wide range of unique web tools as they create compelling and dynamic course environments:

- Multimedia materials, incorporating pictures, graphics, video clips and animations.
- Variety of course content—panel discussions, interviews, guest lectures, debates—offer different perspectives than single-authored textual material.
- Access to a wide range of resources—electronic databases, online libraries, webliographies, and full-text papers.
- Self-assessment questions with feedback, allowing the learner to test their understanding and revise for exams.
- Combining asynchronous tools and communication methods with synchronous events allows a richer environment to be created—one with presence and pacing as well as time for reflection and flexibility of access.

Examples of courses which exploit the potential of the web appear in the literature (e.g., Collis et al., 2002) and on the web (e.g., Koory, 2003). These leading-edge courses are a very long way from printed materials stuck up on the web, and demonstrate that elearning can be an exciting, complex and challenging environment in which to learn.

3. *Enabling learning rather than delivering or directing it.*   Elearning courses at the forefront of pedagogy employ a wide range of active and interactive approaches in the creation of a student-centered learning environment. Some of these involve learner choice in deciding which parts of the course to study in detail; others involve individual personalization of the learning environment. All of them provide activities with which the learner can engage, either individually or in groups. Two examples are: problem-based learning and role-play simulations.

Problem-based learning (PBL) is a widely used approach to course design that uses an instructional problem as the principal vehicle for learning. Jonassen distinguishes between well-structured and ill-structured problems:

> The most commonly encountered problems, especially in schools and universities, are well-structured problems. Well-structured problems typically present all elements of the problem; engage a limited number of rules and principles that are organized in a predictive and prescriptive arrangement; possess correct, convergent answers; and have a preferred, prescribed solution process. These are the kinds of problems that are most often presented in formal education, particularly in mathematics and the sciences. Ill-structured problems, on the other hand, are the kinds of problems that are encountered in everyday practice. Ill-structured problems have many alternative solutions to problems, vaguely defined or unclear goals and constraints, multiple solution paths, and multiple criteria for evaluation solutions; they are more difficult to solve. (Jonassen, 2002, p. 79)

The analysis and study of ill-structured problems take place over several phases and involve both individual and group study. The process has been successfully adapted for the online environment by a number of practitioners (see, e.g., Naidu & Oliver, 1996). Through a number of iterations involving discussion, reflection, commenting, data-gathering and refocusing, the group aims to arrive at a final comment on the problem situation and how they sought to resolve it (Naidu, 2003).

Role-play is another strategy which has been successfully adapted to the online environment. Online role-plays are situations in which learners take on the "characters" of specific people in a contrived educational game. Through playing out these roles, and through the introduction of various events, learners can broaden their perspective, amass a wide knowledge of details through enjoyable activity, and achieve learning outcomes of both an explicit and tacit nature. Students can be organized into teams or take on the role of known characters and respond appropriately through a series of events or crises. In order to play their roles effectively they need to research their characters and the context. Practitioners include Vincent and Shepherd (1998) and Naidu, Ip, and Linser (2000).

In short, these are approaches which invite learners to shed the passive role of knowledge consumers and assume the role of active meaning makers.

MAINSTREAMING ELEARNING

As with all evolutionary processes, it is impossible to say when it began, but most would agree elearning has at least a fifteen-year history already. There is also general agreement that the first phase of elearning is now over; that is, the phase of unrealistic hype, of enthusiastic activity by the early adopters and disdain or ignorance by everyone else.

> We are probably on the end of the early adopter phase and moving more into the mainstream. It is important to remember that e-learning is still a relatively recent phenomenon. In the last several years, we have seen the acceptance of e-learning increase significantly. The thing that causes me to think that we are moving more into mainstream is that people are no longer looking at e-learning as something unusual; it is becoming part of our vocabulary and practice throughout education. (Oblinger, 2003, p. 227)

This transition to the mainstream is exactly what we are advocating—that connectivity must be part of the way we learn. However, there is a danger here: that elearning is simply a new widget, that educators merely regard adding an online element to their courses as all that is required to keep them up-to-date. This business-as-usual attitude to elearning fails to take account of the profound changes that connectivity is producing. In short, the potential of elearning is in danger of being hijacked. As any innovation becomes mainstreamed, it inevitably looses its potential! Nevertheless, there are signs of elearning becoming marginalised before we have investigated its possibilities. Some of these signs are:

- that the elearning agenda is being dictated by the imperative from extrinsically motivated learners who want to get their degree faster, cheaper and more conveniently;
- that the relentless drive for lower-cost options in higher education and training is affecting the quality of online learning;
- that the need for "root and branch" change in higher education is being compromised by the natural human resistance to innovations that require profound change.

On many campuses we see elearning being implemented in a way that undermines the value of both face-to-face *and* online learning. Lecturers continue to lecture, though they put their slides online. Fewer students turn up to the lectures because the slides are online, and because they are working during the day to pay their tuition. This is a lose-lose scenario, for the learner, the instructor and the institution. What is needed at the very minimum, is a rethink of the whole course delivery mechanism. The lecturer needs to look at the curriculum, identify what is already available online and set up a database of useful resources. Then those aspects of the course that really need face-to-face discussion should be identified, and time allocated for seminars and student presentations. Finally, the activities and collaborative work should be laid out on the course website and tools added for students to work together or individually. The leading edge academics on campuses are approaching elearning in this way, but by far the majority are not (Cummings et al., 2002).

The same lackluster approach to elearning can be seen in distance education where print-based content is put online and email contact with the instructor offered. In other cases, hours of lectures are delivered at a distance through either video conferencing or webcasting. Unfortunately, the notion that the results (final marks) are the same regardless of the medium of delivery has provided evidence for the notion that teaching can be transferred from one medium to another without modification. Elearning courses that have been conceived for the online environment, however, show that elearning can produce very positive results (e.g., Kumari, 2001).

PROBLEMS WITH CONNECTED LEARNING

Elearning is not the silver bullet with which all educational problems will be solved. However, the web is the "medium of our time," and learning must take account of its implications.

The immediate drawbacks of elearning have been well documented:

- Online communication is time-consuming and compared to studying a textbook, the outcomes are more diffuse and hard to measure.
- Elearning courses are not cheap alternatives to traditional methods and are even more demanding of instructor resources than the lecture method.
- Students need extra support in moving away from an instructor-led model to a student-centered model of learning. The former tends to be less demanding and the latter require more individual commitment, initiative and self-direction.
- Certain curriculum areas—e.g., the sciences—which have always relied on a linear, building-block approach to instruction, require even more restructuring than humanities subjects when being rethought for the online environment.
- Intellectual property and copyright laws restrict the sharing of information.
- Access to the web is far from universal and high-speed access needed for many of the really innovative applications of elearning is even less available.

Less rehearsed than these limitations are a range of unknowns about the long-term effects of elearning:

- Can the emphasis on process over content eventually lead to courses which lack substance and learners who lack understanding?

- To what extent can the accessibility of information on the internet turn users into overnight experts? Can in-depth study over many years be short circuited?
- What are the implications of effectively endorsing the view that only that which can be digitized is considered to be knowledge?
- How can we anticipate the long-term effects of the consummerization of learning, whereby the learner becomes a customer and learning becomes a commodity to be bought and sold?

These are dangers which we need to track. There will also be the inevitable rogue courses, bad practice in institutional support and corners being cut in the quality of elearning programs, and these will require monitoring and improving.

Another perspective on elearning comes from questioning what it is that we are we losing by adopting elearning. Some of the aspects of this question have already been identified—usually by onlookers who decry the passing of the old ways:

- Loss of the so-called duration of experience (called reverie) in the face of the fragmentation of time in cyberworld.
- A reduced attention span and general impatience with sustained inquiry.
- Abandonment of sustained narrative as a mode of learning.
- Estrangement from geographical place (Birkets, 1994).

Poster (1990) goes so far as to warn about the dispersal of identity through computer networking and the impact this has on social and personal processes. Elearning hastens the move away from a stable body of knowledge, typified by the book, to a world in which information is neither stable nor fixed.

UNDERSTANDING LEARNING IN A CONNECTED WORLD

There is general agreement that we have moved away from the idea of learning as propositional knowledge of that which already exists. But what are we moving toward?

Procedural and performance knowledge are two of the new requirements:

- Knowing as an ability to perform (e.g., how to find and interrogate, how to get things done effectively and especially efficiently).
- Knowing the procedures for making and creating connections between information sources.
- Knowing the ways to both make new moves in a game and to change the very rules of the game.

This directly confronts traditional epistemology that, as concretized in normal science, presupposes stability in the rules of the game as the norm, and paradigm shifts as the exception. (Lankshear, 2003, p. 183)

A third requirement involves the move away from individual knowing. The multidisciplinary team supersedes the notion of the individual expert. As it is impossible for the individual to master all that is known in even a small corner of a subject, information gathering is now organized through dispersed networks of people, services and technologies. Lankshear calls this a collective assemblage involving many minds and machines. Knowing is no longer a property of an individual, but resides in the collective assemblage (Lankshear, 2003, p. 176). In short, there is less emphasis on knowing the truth, and more on networked intelligence.

CONCLUSION

The current advertising slogan of a telecom company says: "More connectivity; more opportunities." Hopefully this chapter has demonstrated that the situation regarding connected learning is much more complex than such a simple slogan implies. Yes, elearning does offer opportunities—in fact, tremendous opportunities if well implemented. But these opportunities come at a price.

Yes, elearning does involve change—in fact, profound change in our attitudes, our roles and our institutions. Yet we live in a world which is dominated by change, and must somehow adapt our learning mechanisms to reflect this.

Yes, we do need to embrace the elearning world, but we must do this with an understanding of the gains and losses, the opportunities and the dangers.

We need creative thinkers, not students of convention and conformity. Received knowledge is losing value in the face of knowledge acquired through individual and group discovery. Connectivity to information needs to be underpinned by critical analysis; connectivity to other people needs to be balanced with self-directed knowledge seeking.

CHAPTER 4

Learning Communities— Entering the Connecticon

INTRODUCTION

Although it has been argued that the increasing spread of access to the information society has challenged the traditional hierarchies of power (Cleveland, 1985), we need to carefully question these assumptions (Kling, 1996). Traditional hierarchies of power are based upon control, secrecy, ownership, and structural disadvantage—to what extent have these really

THE MEANING OF LIFE? SURE, GIVE ME THREE SECONDS

GOOGLE SEARCH

GURU

Source: Robert Thompson, The Guardian.

been dismantled by connectivity? The rapidly changing digital revolution of the "infobahn" (Negroponte, 1995) may indeed loosen individuals from to the bonds of a single geographical community. It may also help to provide a greater choice for rural and remote geographical communities, enabling the participants to extend their social and commercial interactions from a purely local to a global scale. It may also be true, as Cleveland (1985) suggests that in the future knowledge economy "civilisation will be built around communities of people, and less around communities of place," but these assumptions have important implications for minority interests and geographical communities of place whose citizens are still on the margins of this digital civilization, whether it is by lack of infrastructure, training, or any other ability to fully participate in the digital society.

A growing number of governments are emphasizing the importance of a role for online political communities of interest to shape the policies and practices of democratic decision-making (Ascherson, 2003 and Koert, 2002). Does it always follow that greater participatory decision-making will result from the provision of a greater availability of information? If this information is more easily accessible, and structured to include serious feedback and participant interactivity as standard operating procedures, will it mean better democracy? Or will the growth of online communities simply mean ever greater volumes of information swilling around the Connecticon with the various interest groups (politicians, civil servants, business people, lobbyists etc.) developing ways of circumventing disclosure, managing information, and inventing new hegemonies (Birdsall, 1999)? Will the digital divide be less about Internet access and more about the gulf between the people who are able to learn how to manage digital information in the global repository of the Connecticon, and those who cannot?

THE SPREAD OF TELECENTRES

Before we get down to these questions, and the benefits or disbenefits of learning in a connected society, we should spend a little time retracing the growth of online communities and their involvement with our social system, especially in the fields of education and commerce. We do not need to start at the beginning of the Internet as there are plenty of good accounts and analyses of the early experiences (e.g., Rheingold, 2000 and Castells, 2001). It is the community applications that we are concerned with here.

By the mid 1980s the potential had been realized in the Nordic countries to establish a number of Community Teleservice Centres (to give them their full name) usually called telecottages because of their prime purpose to provide telecommunications services in rural and isolated areas. These telecottages aimed to give public access to data processing and other computer-assisted services in order to counteract some geographically determined disadvantages that affected the local community (Qvortrup, 1989). They were intended to offer communal use, either to people in the village who wanted to drop in to do some computer assisted work (word processing, spreadsheet management, sending electronic mail) or in some cases to provide a desk and facilities for an employee working at a distance from the headquarters of their employment. A key element in the growth of the telecottages network was a belief that their establishment could form part of a positive strategy for rural and regional development (Bryden et al., 1993 and Sandler, 1999). In Denmark and Sweden the telecottages were largely looked upon as public institutions— they were frequently called "electronic village halls"—and consequently a high priority was given to educational activities, both on-site instruction and via distance education tutorials. In Norway and Sweden telecottages were frequently private establishments, independent of public authorities.

From the beginning three issues were recognized as crucially important, these being:

1. The need to establish an electronic infrastructure to enable greater access;
2. The need to build linked networks to overcome the difficulties of isolation and promote decentralization of regional development activities;
3. The need to integrate learning and doing in a variety of different sectors, including education, teleworking, and the provision of electronic services (but with a clear distinction that it should be a communal activity in fellowship, rather than "home-working").

In the intervening twenty years these points have continually been reemphasized as priorities for Connecticon networks around the globe. As they have developed, Community Teleservice Centres (CTC) have by-and-large continued their multipurpose function, but they have divided into two main groups. These can be seen as the CTC that are primarily:

> directed towards the public, providing educational training facilities, social services and the like, and there are others which are oriented more towards business life, supporting local enterprises, or themselves working as small enterprises. (Qvortrup, 1994)

Many of course have continued to attempt to provide both educational and business services, and the structures for achieving these different functions have often proved to be difficult, innovative and/or highly revealing about the attitudes of different societies toward work, education, and the freedom of information. Gomez and others (1999) agreed with the broad rationale of promoting support for the dispersal of increased access to high quality information and communications technologies (ICT) as part of strategies to stimulate sustainable development in rural areas, and they proposed a typology of five types of telecentre experiences or models.

1. The basic telecentre—generally located in rural or marginalized areas where the population has limited access to ICT services in general. A key ingredient for their success is the training of operators and people from the local communities who are the potential users.

2. The telecentre franchise—a series of interconnected telecentres that are usually centrally coordinated but independently owned and operated. Essentially a small business normally directed toward providing public access.

3. The Civic Telecentre—Probably the most common but hardest to classify, including public libraries, schools, universities, community organizations and other civic institutions. Often quite low key as the telecentre services and access are simply offered in addition to their other public service provision.

4. Cybercafe—a growing number of "drop-in" centers that cater mainly for tourists, young people, and business people on the move, often just to check e-mail, send a fax or surf the Web for short-term information. These are increasingly being found in hotel foyers, shopping malls, train stations, airports etc. and are increasingly common in locations where connectivity is a problem—less developed countries, and isolated rural areas of more developed countries.

5. Multipurpose Community Telecentre—a sort of Rolls Royce version of the other types, sometimes specializing in functions such as telemedicine or distance learning, but usually with a very wide range of other services, including business, public agency, and ICT consultancy roles.

In all of these different types the opportunities for learning, either online or offline, formal or non-formal, tend to be very varied. This search for variety and the local application to a niche that encourages usability and sustainability has led to the burgeoning of slight modifications on these five different types, often going under a multiplicity of different names (teleservice centers, telecentres, telecottages, community technology centers, community communication shops, networked (or local) learning centers, community access points, digital clubhouses, multipurpose telecentres, community business centers, etc.)

The spread of local telecentres now includes not simply the more remote corners of the Western "developed" world, but also facilities of various sorts throughout Australasia, Africa (Owen & Darkwa, 2000 and Gitta & Ikoja-Odongo, 2003), South America, and various parts of Asia (Latchem & Walker, 2001). In Europe and North America they still tend to be located in the more rural and remote areas of country, but as any rural geographer will tell you, these terms are relative. There is a wide spectrum of context for the location of telecentres, from simply decentralized buildings that allow access to centralized resources over a wide geographical area of Germany (Bernath et al., 2003) to much more isolated locations in Australia (Share, 1993), Canada (Latchem & Walker, 2001), and Central Europe (ITU, 1998).

Despite this wide variety in the nomenclature, styles and functions of telecentres, and the understanding of their role in the processes of education and development, there is some common ground. There is a general recognition that the most important feature of a telecentre is that it is in some way supporting local community activities, in particular by utilizing modern information technology to strengthen the cohesion of local communities in rural areas (Falch, in ITU, 1998, pp. 173–181). To a large extent these different models need only concern us in passing, as there is a wide overlap in the activities that any individual might engage within any one telecentre, and anyway, as we shall explore in the following chapter, the spread of faster access through broader bandwidth is likely to alter the roles of telecentres even further. As the ability to secure faster and more accurate Internet access from home and small businesses becomes more readily available then we will need to question why local people might want to use telecentres at all. It might be because they are able to get more peace to work than being at home with the family, or it may be to meet socially with others who are studying and working in a similar environment, or it may be to access certain specialist pieces of equipment that are still too expensive to be widespread for domestic use, but it will not be, as in the past, simply because the telecentre is the only show in town that allows Internet access.

LEARNING BY DOING

In the broadest sense, each of these telecentres is contributing to education, in the general sense by sharing information and communications between a network of people, separated by time and/or distance. In a more specific context the telecentres aim to unleash the untapped potential of the people (for personal and local development), help to organize regional resources and expertise, foster the emergence of local capability, and promote a comprehensive approach to servicing the multiple of needs (Owen & Darkwa, 2000). Some of the most common business models for telecentres are partnership arrangements (Falch, in ITU, 1998) such as:

1. integration with local institutions (schools, libraries, training centers etc.);
2. service provision for local authorities or regional government;

3. service provision for local small businesses and voluntary organizations;
4. provision of public access facilities (Internet cafes, drop-in centers etc.);
5. teleworking facilities for distributed companies.

Like all new technologies the opportunities also come with threats of a downside, and one's perspective depends on which side of the technology gap one is standing. The introduction of new technology allows the local actors to become part of the global arena, but also enables them to bypass established local connections. For example, consumers may decide to shop online rather than order the same product locally; students may chose to study at home, but via a bigger university further away; workers may work from home (or closer-to-home) rather than spend hours each day traveling to and from 'local' work.

Globalization generally has been seen to have both positive and negative outcomes, especially in that many of the potentially positive outcomes are not realized in practice. The globalization of education is no exception to this rule. Despite the value of global education in offering diversity of choice, this comes at the expense of encouraging local initiatives which value local culture and promote national beliefs, skills and knowledge. The potential power of globalized teaching to spread dominant ideologies and to crush emerging structures, whether wittingly or unwittingly, is a cause for concern. Cunningham and colleagues noted in 1997 a rising level of concern in Asia over the loss of identity, culture and family values due to the availability of global education (Cunningham et al., 1998).

COMMUNITY NETWORKS

Though there are swings and roundabouts to the adoption of new technology as an educational tool (or a development strategy) the spectacular growth of Internet use is a fact that even ardent opponents have to recognize (Edwards & Usher, 2000). This growth presents both threats and opportunities (Manniche & Marcussen, 1997) that we have to take into account, and necessitate the adoption of some new pedagogical concepts (Bernath et al., 2003). It is clear that however good the networks may be, their technological brilliance alone is not enough to guarantee their use and survival. A major factor, though difficult to quantify, is the extent to which the network is able to facilitate a social interchange between users, and this has been a driver in the growth of online support facilities, self-help groups, online gaming, and shop-with-a-friend applications. More specifically, we think there are lessons in the study of community networks that shed interesting light on the processes of engagement and interaction of "ordinary" people using computer-based networks.

We use the term "community networks" for physical communities of people who have chosen to utilize information and communications technology to deploy integrated solutions to the problems of information dissemination, knowledge exchange, and group interactivity. This interactivity typically includes e-mail access, Web-based information and directories, listservers, chat rooms, and local new or information services. Frequently there may also be advanced services such as Internet radio, voice-over-IP (a sort of internet telephone), videoconferencing, and video streaming facilities. Koert (2002) and others (Swan, 2002) have emphasized that "interactivity is probably the single most relevant and characteristic feature of networked electronic media" and linked this to the dynamic of greater participation in development, democratic behavior, and in entrepreneurial activity. This is certainly reflected in the development of community networks (Cohill & Kavanaugh, 2000). In the establishment of the Blacksburg community network in Virginia (Blacksburgh, 2000 and Carroll & Rosson, 1996) we see a clear development path that other, more recent community networks have adopted and adapted.

Blacksburg, Virginia

A common scenario consists of local champions, often from public agencies taking the lead in establishing the backbone of a network. In the case of Blacksburg the project was initially hosted by the university, which formed a partnership with the local telephone company (Bell Atlantic) and the Town of Blacksburg. Gradually the network was extended and moved to a nonprofit community business, with the interests of the whole community as a priority (Cohill, 2002). Critical mass was built up by partnerships including the local government, schools, libraries, a telecommunications company, as well as local businesses and voluntary organizations. Each of these constituents may have had slightly different needs and aspirations from a community network, but a major breakthrough came with the realization that this had become an educational project rather than a technology project (Cohill, 2000). As local schools became connected to the network the university group began to train school teachers and others to use the Internet. Significantly, as the focus on education increased, more and more Blacksburg residents began to register for the network services. Although the most heavily used area of the network Web site is the Village Mall, a central directory of all business in the area, the network architects were careful to include home owners and other properties in the expansion of the network. The result is a claim of more than 87% of the town's residents connected to the network, and suggestions that it is America's (or the world's) "most wired town."

The extent of interaction and to some extent the success of the network can be judged by facts such as:

- the doubling of visits to the library after Internet access was available,
- the number of community organizations and civic groups that have reported that when they go online their attendance at meetings goes up,
- by the reports that when people are online they tend to get more involved in community affairs and to feel closer to other people in the community.

We have heard this story time and time again when we visit community networks and speak with the users. Similarly, we have noted the close link between the vitality of a community network and the strength of its links with educational activities, whether formal courses on "using the Internet" or non-formal "learning from each other" bootstrap development. It is not enough simply to put a large volume of information on the Web and hope people will use it. Cohill (2000) proposes a partnership model for the development of community networks that cite at least nine different groups in the community as having an important role to play. These are:

1. The media, including local newspapers, magazines, local television and local radio. (Although the media often seems to see community networks as a threat and open hostility is not uncommon).

2. Local government and other agencies require large amounts of high quality services and are both customers and suppliers of information on the network.

3. Community and civic groups are key beneficiaries of low-cost Internet services, and in their turn contribute a high value to the social context of the network.

4. Schools and educational institutions have an important two-way relationship in the provision of access and training for networking.

5. Libraries are often a key network resource in the community, and in some subject areas the immediacy and accessibility of Web-based resources have taken over from conventional books and reports.

6. Individual residents utilize the network for personal use, as well as in their capacity as members of local organizations and businesses.

7. Health care providers, including doctors, hospitals, and nursing homes is often a popular and important area of community network activity.

8. Telecommunication companies and local Internet service providers may be useful partners or may regard the network as competition,

and the distinction may be in the size and ownership structure of the company.

9. Local businesses can all benefit from working with the community network, with both suppliers and customers using the network for trading, and simply exchanging information.

Although the Blacksburg model is one of the best-developed and longest running community networks, there are others (Riedel et al., 1998).

Upper Karelia, Finland

The Learning Upper Karelia Project in Finland is an initiative in using local and rural information networking in an attempt to prevent social exclusion, support social innovations, and improve services and living conditions in the region (Oksa & Turuuen, 2000). Most of the project activities focused on creating and supporting local capabilities for using computers and networks. More than 30 computer kiosks were established as free access points for the Internet and home visits were encouraged to install software and train new users. The Public sector began to produce information the network and information about local enterprises and civic organizations was also included. The project sought to deliver its goals through developing new forms of social cooperation together with the mobilization of unused human resources—some unemployed young people were trained and employed as trainers and support people for the community network (Oksa, 2001). The construction of a community information network was seen as an important tool for local and regional development, and the success of the initial project has resulted in several other pilot projects in different parts of Finland. Keys to the success of the initiative are considered to be the skillful connection between the development needs of the locality and the opportunities offered through the process of developing networked learning. Local partnership arrangements were important, including the problem-centred local style of implementation. The project concluded that information technology projects need non-technological (e.g., social) objectives, and that the project was a learning process in itself linking local resources and local needs to the wider issues affecting that society.

Educational Communities

Headquartered in Sudbury and Thunder Bay, Contact North facilitates access to education and training opportunities offered by Northern

Ontario's colleges, universities and school boards. Using audioconferencing, videoconferencing, audiographics and Internet technologies, Contact North uses 145 Access Centres which provide courses to more than 100 small and remote communities. Twenty-three of these communities can only be reached by air and most have no other post-secondary presence. The Access Centres are hosted by the local communities as an indication of their commitment to educational opportunities. In return, Contact North provides the technology, telephone lines, the cost of transmission, staff to schedule courses and assist students, as well as a variety of other services for students and the educational providers.

The community of Cochrane is just one example of the kind of small, remote town served by Contact North. Its population is less than 5,500 but it provides several Access Centres: one in the local secondary school, a videoconference facility in the local library and two smaller centers in the town offices and the post office. In 2002, 324 students took 71 courses including 10 full-time programs and 9 part-time courses. Contact North is funded directly by the Ontario government that regards the program as an important part of its strategy of meeting the needs of people in the North.

Professional Communities

Gurstein (1999) highlighted some of the opportunities for ICT to support local economic development, in particular by:

- enabling local residents to do their work more efficiently and therefore maintain their competitive edge in the wider market.
- providing new businesses and new styles of business.
- linking the community into larger networks to achieve economies of scale.

Not only does this support allow the nature and structure of business organizations to be completely reshaped, he notes that it allows these flexible networks to:

gain advantage from geographic or cultural social distinctiveness and from being a component of a larger network of producers, even when the linkages are largely "virtual." (Gurstein, 1999, p. 7)

This does not just include teleworkers, but also allows small firms, located in a particular place, to aggregate their work in a manner that optimizes their selective advantages. The network is used to permit continuous communication, work sharing, remote administration and management, and to present a single "front door" to the world for marketing etc. The small firms can remain small while obtaining the benefits of belonging to a larger organization.

In a comparative analysis of face-to-face and computer-mediated communities it was noted (Etzioni & Etzioni, 1999) that a hybrid type of community that is based on a combination of face-to-face and online communications is particularly effective in bonding and sharing its values. Many businesses seem attracted to the idea of being involved in an online community. Frequently it appears to be just another way to market their products, though the more interactive Web sites that encourage feedback and foster the trust of participants appear to have a stronger community identity (Boyd, 2002). Despite a large number of quality publications on the techniques of design and usability of the supporting structure of online communities (Preece, 2000 and Kim, 2000) both for learning and for business, there is no guaranteed way to develop a successful community. There is, however, general agreement that the architecture of a community, particularly how the software allows the participants to interact, is an important element influencing the way in which a community develops.

Werry (1999) has reviewed the concept of community in a business context and notes that "the figure of a dynamic, partially 'self-organising' ecosystem is perhaps the most pervasive means of representing virtual communities." This is where community networks have an added advantage, combining the social and communications benefits of both physical geographical communities and distributed communities online (McInnes, 1997). As in other communities the residents of Telluride, Colorado felt that their community network had increased communication between residents, but significantly, although the network was well used as a discussion forum, they found no evidence that the technology necessarily led to a more democratic society. The network provides discussion groups and a forum for communication for the physical community that helps to enhance that sense of community, but other factors such as user motivation, equality of access and skills confidence will also affect just how inclusive the community network can claim to be.

The Community of Citizens

In the larger context it is worth looking at another type of community network, the community of the nation, for most online communities are self-selecting and while physical communities of place may be determined by residence, kinship etc., they are normally relatively small scale (Fox & Roberts, 1999). While many agree that the global networked community offers the potential of greater online democratic participation, it has also been argued that the Web is becoming less egalitarian, more institutionally based, and more commercially driven each day that passes (Riley et al., 1998 and Evans, 2000). In an examination of "cyberspace and the concept of democracy" Evans (2000) concluded that the emergent property of the Internet to act as a host to a wide variety of voices (opinions) and to support a relationship among these voices, is an important basis from which to view democracy as a form of life. He warns against the danger of restricting the number of voices that can be heard, and a reduction in the intensity of their interplay in favor of a single, dominant "oracle" that dictates the institutional (or corporate) line. This agrees well with Dabinett's thoughts on grassroot community development and ICT that:

> the ownership and regulation of ICT infrastructure, services, and applications should become a key contested area for community economic development. (Dabinett, 2000, p. 164)

As a tangent, Rheingold (2000, p. 216) speculates that the current tendency of Internet users to tolerate a wide diversity of opinion might be a limiting factor in promoting the inclusivity of a global Internet community, and that "fragmentation, hierarchization, rigidifying social boundaries, and single-niche colonies of people who share intolerances could become prevalent in the future."

In this context it is revealing to look at some Scottish experiments with electronic democracy (Ascherson, 2003). The revival of the Scottish Parliament in 1999 after nearly 300 years of suspension and amalgamation within the UK Parliament has led to a wide range of initiatives to bring a greater level of democratic participation, power-sharing, and decision-making transparency to the new political processes in Scotland. Four main areas of ICT in governance have been identified.

- **E-government**—using the Internet principally as an electronic notice board.
- **E-Community**—such as the provision by a public authority of a network of Internet access points in public places through which community members are encouraged to follow their own interests.
- **Electronic Village Halls**—a community facility in which local people can have free access to ICT kit and get help to use it.
- **E-Democracy**—a family of projects sharing the aim of using the new media to enhance democracy by opening the structure of government to much closer scrutiny and by enabling the public some active part in shaping policies.

The Scottish Parliament has become a world leader in the application of digital technology to enhance participatory democracy, but despite an impressive range of "e-experiments" (including webcasting, interactive discussion boards, and e-petitions) there is still a crucial mismatch between the offer of participation and the level of uptake. Only a small minority of the Scottish public make use of the services, and even with rapid growth through wider and faster access to the Internet, it can be expected that a political e-underclass will develop. The e-Democracy experiments are still at an early stage, and making predictions in any technology-related area is notoriously dangerous. Will e-democracy take root, or will it be misappropriated by existing power structures? Alternatively, it may be totally ignored by a society increasingly alienated by political processes.

WHAT MAKES A SUCCESSFUL COMMUNITY NETWORK?

Key conclusions from these experiments are that it is possible for communities to project something of their own identity into an online environment, and the critical importance of interaction among community members is crucial to the life and vitality of the network. It is also recognized, however, that computer-mediated communication is not inherently interactive (Swan, 2002) and requires a social environment that facilitates as well as encourages peer-to-peer interaction, frequently facilitated by mentors or tutors. Cohill (2000) from his work at Blacksburg and elsewhere has suggested nine challenges for community networks. In summary, they are as follows.

- **The changing rights to information—who owns information and who can distribute it?** Whether it is the transfer of music, text, or simply ideas on discussion boards, information can be money to some companies and they may seek to control its distribution and use. In community networks, however, there is an imperative to make information freely and easily available in order to encourage transparent, democratic decision-making as well as to foster individual and group creativity.
- **The right to communicate as a basic principle of citizenship** (echoed by Birdsall, 1999) is an extension of the liberal Western concept of "freedom of speech" and when it is under threat from any restriction then we may need to establish community-managed networks to provide public fora for community and civic discussions. This conflict of interest has led some community networks to call for networks to be managed by municipal authorities as another service (like water, sewage disposal, schools, roads etc.). A comparison might be reliance on the state to provide an efficient postal service that does not tolerate censorship of personal or business mail.

- **Privacy issues, especially as they relate to personal information and the needs of the community for open communication.** This is a related issue and refers not just to the contents of messages, but issues such as personal information being collected on users without their knowledge or consent. This "user profiling" may include user "tracking" (following the Web sites you have accessed or individuals you have made contact with) as well as collecting "horizontal" data not related to your initial inquiry (such as integrating users bank details with their health records and a record of their credit card purchases).

- **The issue of who should own telecommunications infrastructure,** and how communities can ensure a sustainable future by prudent investment is a fundamental issue for most community networks. We have heard this voiced in a number of communities as a concern. Even in rural communities that have established independent local networks precisely because the big telecommunication companies are not interested in small numbers of isolated users, the formation of a rival local network frequently seems to provoke a belated reaction from the big telecom supplies to offer its services. It is at this point the tension is most acute. Can the community network extend its role and become sustainable? Will partnership with the bigger company mean loss of autonomy and higher costs? This dilemma has led many communities to call for the adoption of the community network as a basic municipal service and to aggregate with other community networks to seek solidarity and influence.

- **The confusion over knowledge vs. information and the ability of citizens to transform information to knowledge** are a common educational concern. The argument centers on the difference between learning information and mechanical skills versus learning *where* to find information and learning *how* to learn in order to reconstruct knowledge into understanding in a range of different and unpredictable situations. This theme is central to the book.

- **Changing relationship between government and citizen.** The enormous volume of information available, and the ease of access via electronic networks means that there is no longer any excuse for citizens not being informed, nor for public bodies not to inform the citizens. This does not come without problems of course, especially sorting the enormous volume of potential information into a relevant and useable format, but the process has started and we need to see much more experimentation on new approaches to local governance.

- **Leadership crisis** (at every level) is resulting in a failure to address the issues raised by increasing globalization of business and the impact this is having on local businesses. Not only are transnational

retail corporations now in direct competition with many local businesses, the mobility of their career structure is actually encouraging
the depletion of intellectual and social capital in rural areas as progressive employees are shuffled around the corporation like cogs in a
wheel. This area offers important opportunities for decentralized key
workers to become teleworkers, and for elearning as part of staff
development planning.

- **Decision-making crisis** (in top-down hierarchical decision-making
  systems) is at least partly as a result of continued adherence to older
  ways of working that do not take cognisance of the new opportunities
  and demands of an interconnected, hyperactive, global society. Flat-
  ter managerial structures, opportunities for collaborative working,
  and learning programs that enable students to become tutors in a
  peer-to-peer learning process are some examples of networked solutions to this problem.

- **A future orientation** to encourage a forward-looking agenda rather
  than necessarily dwelling on systems that worked for a previous generation is an important component of working and learning in a network connected society. In the next chapter we consider ways in
  which working practices have been changed to take advantage of
  these new opportunities and develop a construction that may help us
  to optimize the benefits of change.

While many of these issues go well beyond the scope of this book, they
cannot be disregarded completely, and the complex, integrated nature of
the interlacing system of networks calls for some radical rethinking—not
just of what is possible, but of what we should be aiming for as a learning
society. A critical role for communities networks in the next twenty years or
so is to create and maintain public spaces in the Connecticon. This can be
achieved not only by adopting a public (municipal or state government)
role in the construction and support of the first level of the Connecticon,
the hardware and linkages (wires, fibers, satellites or radio transmitters)
but also by nurturing the second level, the human resource that will use
these networks. Cohill (2000) concluded that there are six key roles to be
played by community networks. These roles revolve around a commitment
to serious investment in community networks in order to develop a com-
munity-owned infrastructure, enabling support for community economic
development initiatives micro-businesses (less than 10 employees), and
SME's (small and medium-sized enterprises). Additional roles he suggested are to provide public spaces on the network where citizens can
exchange news and information, to facilitate the training and skills development needed to enable individuals to cope with these changes creatively,
and lastly to help to extend the level of community publishing (text, voice,

video, radio, and other multimedia) to develop and sustain the opportunities to share information constructively and creatively.

CONCLUSIONS

The Internet has long been hailed as the "peoples' medium," leapfrogging over traditional power structures and providing access to information for the traditionally information-poor and a voice to the traditionally silent majority. In this chapter we have examined a number of ways in which this prophecy is being fulfilled: access to educational opportunities through the growth of telecentres, the rise of community networks and the advent of e-democracy. However, it would be over-optimistic to regard these directions as anything but the tip of a very large iceberg. Furthermore, there are signs that some of these initiatives are falling on stony ground: the take-up of educational opportunities is not always self-sustaining; community networks can languish unused by the majority, and e-democracy has yet to attract significant users. Local educational providers can be undercut by global providers and many initiatives are dependent on continued funding.

Nevertheless, from the projects which are successful it is evident that online community and online learning can be powerful change agents.

CHAPTER 5

Connecting with High Speed Internet Access

INTRODUCTION

The term broad-band, refers to a new generation of high-speed transmission services aimed at residential and small business users. It is a generic term used in relation to a number of technologies for delivering fast data communications ser-vices. However, there is

"When I told him we need to increase our bandwidth, he hired six fat tuba players."

no agreed threshold that marks the boundary between broadband and nar-rowband. A recent National Research Center study claims that "various groups have struggled to develop appropriate definitions of broadband, and these definitions have changed over time" (National Research Coun-cil, 2002).

Communications capacity or speed, is only one of the characteristics that define broadband. Another way of distinguishing broadband—at least from dial-up access—is "always-on" connectivity. There are also other

The Connecticon: Learning for the Connected Generation, pages 65–78

parameters such as bandwidth symmetry between upstream and down-stream capacity, latency or delay in how long it takes to deliver a packet across the network and addressability. All of these aspects have implications for the types of services that can appropriately be deployed over broad-band. Video-on-demand and other streaming media applications rely on the availability of downstream bandwidth, while information appliances require always-on service though the bandwidth requirement is low. The total broadband use in a home may be made up of multiple applications being used simultaneously by different family members. This is relevant to elearning applications which are unlikely to be the primary reason for ini-tial broadband take-up but will piggyback on a range of other uses of broadband in the home.

Experience of new technology deployment over many years makes clear that it is the social structures and human processes that need to be re-engi-neered before the transformative potential of the new technology can be realized (Daniel, 2002). As changing human processes and evolving social structures are much harder to effect than installing technology, new initia-tives tend to grind to a halt after the easy part has been accomplished. However, it is too simplistic to blame "technology push" as the cause of many failures in the take-up of technology-based innovations. This is very clear in the case of broadband where the classic dilemma pertains. The technology needs to be in place before people see how they might use it and before services are created to attract users, yet making the technology available is inevitably a technology-led operation.

Educational institutions are notoriously conservative organizations and though elearning is currently the innovative face of most universities and colleges, designing online courses and events specifically for a broadband market seems to be too speculative a venture for such public-funded bod-ies. So the implementation and take up of broadband technology move in fits and starts.

Following roughly a decade of development and experimentation and a recent period of rapid growth, first-generation broadband services, using primarily cable modems and digital subscriber lines, are available in many markets. This progress is offset by recent business failures and uncertainty about the pace of future investment—factors that in part reflect slow growth in subscriptions of broadband services (National Research Council, 2002).

For rural subscribers in particular, broadband provides higher-perfor-mance options in connecting to familiar Internet and other online ser-vices. However, its enhanced capacity and 'always on' nature enable new networked activities which are largely undeveloped. Evaluations of broad-band projects (Lynch, 2000; Sage Research, 2002) generally recognize that true exploitation of high-speed connectivity is in its infancy.

Despite the advertised benefits of broadband connection to the Internet (BT, 2003), there are currently very few actual examples in the UK of these benefits manifesting themselves in the business practices of small businesses, community organizations, or remote locations. After all the hype has been stripped away, it is important to analyze real examples of the potential benefits. Like all new technology, there will be gains and losses for society in general and the users in particular. In part, the paucity of examples illustrating how broadband access has changed the culture of business or educational practice stems from the relatively low uptake outwith the urban, corporate business, and academic networks. This is due to both its relatively high cost and complex technical problems in the provision of ubiquitous access. Underlying this restricted uptake is an understandable confusion surrounding new technology, new definitions, and untested working practices.

For the purposes of this discussion, we will use the definition of broadband suggested by the National Research Council:

> Broadband services should provide sufficient performance—and wide enough penetration of services reaching that performance level—to encourage the development of new applications. (National Research Council, 2002, p. 8)

As the report confirms, this definition implies an evolutionary path that is both technical and economic, in which the last link to the individual user is regarded as a potential bottleneck that inhibits innovation and constrains the development of new services elsewhere in the network.

BROADBAND APPLICATIONS

It has been noted that one of the paradoxes of broadband is that while there is unanimity of agreement that broadband is highly desirable, and everyone should have it, few can identify what it is *really* good for (the so-called killer app) and the take up of it by the public so far has been rather desultory (Odlyzko, 2003). The ultimate form of broadband connectivity currently is fibre, which offers the prospect of almost endlessly upgradeable bandwidth over the same physical link. However, fibre-to-the-home is currently regarded as unfeasible, and residential broadband is usually supplied through cable modems and DSL.

The early adopters of broadband provide classic examples of the power of the Connecticon to bring about economic, social and educational change. The following case studies are illustrative.

Reversing Rural Decline

South Dundas, a rural Canadian township located an hour south of Ottawa, has a population of about 11,000 and consists of several small villages. Throughout the 1990s its economy was in decline and more than 600 jobs were lost in the ten years prior to 2000. A decision was eventually made by the Township to invest in a fibre network to enable the community to connect with new markets. The fibre layout installed in 2001 covered most of the commercial, industrial and community service users in the three main villages with sufficient capacity to anticipate future needs.

Over a period of two years, at least 62 new jobs were created which could be directly attributed to the fibre network. More than $2.8 million was invested in the township in commercial or industrial expansion and $140,000 in increased revenues or decreased costs was credited to the new network (Strategic Networks Group, 2003). Examples of broadband applications in the area of training included online product training for retail sales staff and certification courses for insurance agents. Other uses involved the ability to compete with larger competitors, ease and speed of connection with Head Office, and time-savings leading to greater efficiency and then to expansion of the business.

However, a standard return on investment calculation does not provide an adequate picture of the benefits the Township has gained from the broadband infrastructure. Improvements not directly attributable to the network have taken place because of a new proactive attitude in the community, ensuring its future as a place where people choose to live and work. The local theater has been rescued from closure and now regularly attracts a full house; the local country inn is offering community pay-per-use access to the Internet and hopes to become a local learning center for online education courses.

Providing Municipal Services

The town of Tillsonburg in southern Ontario implemented an award-winning broadband network in 1999 which actually saved money, provided better services to the community and held the line on local taxes. Key to the economic success of the project was the restructuring of services and personnel: for example, eliminating incompatibilities within departments such as the use of five different accounting systems, and reducing the town's outdated corporate structure. Another important building block in the success of the implementation, was the leadership of the senior administrators and elected officials, who made a point of 'leading by example' in the adoption of the new technology. They reduced the number of their council members from nine to five and eliminated all existing standing committees. This served as motivation for staff to embrace change and seek ways to utilize technology to drive efficiencies. A significant commitment to initial and ongoing staff training was made by the town, and this was considered to have resulted in significant efficiency gains. Each member of staff develops a training curriculum, beginning with identifying existing skills and desired skills and job specific applications they would like to learn.

One of the main benefits of the implementation for the residents of Tillsonburg was the opening of the Customer Service Center, which became the focal point for licensing, billings, permits etc. and due to the efficiencies of a "one stop shop," the available service hours were increased by more than 50%. Customer complaints are now tracked electronically through to resolution. Moving from paper to electronic data capturing increased efficiency and reduced workloads. In addition a new telephone system was implemented that centralized all numbers into one dedicated phone number routed through the Customer Service Center. Residents can access the Service Center in person, by phone or through the Web portal. The library provides free Internet access and residents can participate in a range of democratic processes via the Web.

The broadband application in Tillsonburg relied on more than the technology for its success—staff restructuring, leadership and training all contributed to the project. The broadband network was certainly necessary but not sufficient to bring about the changes that have been well documented (http://www.broadband.gc.ca).

Coordinating a County

Simcoe County is one of the largest fibre optic broadband community networks in Canada. The public institutions in virtually every community throughout this largely rural County are connected to each other and to the Internet. Through the private sector, broadband is now being extended to businesses. A total of 680 kilometers of fibre optic cable connects municipal government, health care providers, schools and college campuses, libraries and hospitals. The aim is to create jobs and business opportunities, as well as to give residents electronic access to a wide range of services. Some of the key applications are: a Virtual Town Hall for edemocracy, Surgical Pre-Admission Clinic and Telemedicine applications of patient assessment, consultations, education and meetings, and connectivity for schools and libraries.

Key factors in the success of this—and most other broadband implementations—are:

- A high degree of stakeholder engagement within and from interested communities and a well-established stakeholder team.
- The needs, applications and benefits clearly defined and linked to a vision of community sustainability.
- Extensive experience of project leaders with ICT or community economic development activities.
- Broadband viewed as a strategic asset and enabler, not just a service.

These three examples from Ontario demonstrate the way in which providing outstanding levels of connectivity has far reaching results.

THE ECOLOGY OF THE CONNECTICON

We suggest that our notion of the Connecticon, and in particular broadband access to the Connecticon, resembles a complex adaptive system, an organizational structure with many connections and parts that adapt due to feedback mechanisms that give it the ability to change and survive in a fluctuating environment. It has in fact an ecology of connectivity—a scientific system of the relationships and interactions between the human resources (users) and the totality of their online environment. Like all complex adaptive systems the organization of the Connecticon has characteristic behaviors called emergent properties that function synergistically at each level of the organization to give the system a life that is greater than the sum of its parts (Marten, 2001). Three fundamental emergent properties of the Connecticon are:

1. Self organization
2. Stability domains
3. Complex system cycles

Self-organization

A key process of assembly of complex adaptive systems (social systems and natural systems) is their self-organizating properties known as community assembly. In terms of the Connecticon this is translated as the ability of the system to expand, contract, and adapt structural changes through the process of fitting the parts together—in other words the compatibility and convergence of the various elements of the system. In part this is determined by technical features—whether one machine can communicate effectively to another, or if software can be understood and adapted. Another part of the assembly process is in the area of convenience—new technical solutions, even if they are more efficient, may fail if they do not meet the needs and abilities of their users, the human resource level of the Connecticon. New networks (or subsystems of Connecticon space) may be added or removed from the system, not simply because their users want them to be, but because their "ecological niche" in this complex adaptive system is either realized, or rejected by the ability of the new network to be incorporated within the larger system. This leads us neatly to the emergent property of stability domains.

Stability Domains

In a complex adaptive system there is a constant fluctuation at the sub-system level between the forces that exert a positive feedback (to promote change) and those that exert a negative feedback (resist change and promote stability). The overall balance of the tension between these processes will determine whether the complex adaptive system as a whole will grow, maintain a steady state, or decline. In terms of the Connecticon, the ecosystem state (the overall state of the system) will be influenced by a very wide range of factors, not simply the technological possibilities, but also culture, social values, human perceptions, education, and understanding. It is a complex mix that varies for a particular time, place, and part of the Connecticon system, but the mixture plays a determining factor in whether the whole system maintains a constant level of activity or makes rapid leaps forwards. In both levels of stability there are enormous opportunities for the construction of new knowledge, the combination of knowledge to raise new levels of understanding, and of course opportunities to capitalize upon this new understanding in an entrepreneurial manner that may further change the perceptions, values, and social habits of human society.

Complex System Cycles

A key element in understanding stability domains lies in the emergent property of complex system cycles. It is this property that results in progressive change of the system or sudden switches in direction. In Connecticon terms it could be reflected in the steady rise in numbers of users of email and of the world wide Web; it could be in the sudden and dramatic growth of mobile phone users; it could be the ubiquitous desire of businesses to have a Web presence, or it could be the collapse of dot.com companies on the stock exchange. In educational terms and in our context with particular relevance for how businesses learn to change and innovate, we need to consider whether these system cycles are truly new, or if they are simply a new expression of long established cycles of learning and understanding.

There are four properties specific to broadband access that are challenging the constraints of "traditional" learning and are resulting in new forms of entrepreneurial activity.

1. It is many times faster.
2. It allows transfer of more complex data.
3. It enables much greater interactivity between users (hyper-interactivity).
4. It is always on (avoiding dial up connections and line sharing).

In the following UK case studies we look at each of these features in turn and explore the implications of the technology shift for elearning (electronic learning or enhanced learning is it is being called in some areas) (Reynolds, Caley, & Mason, 2002).

FASTER ACCESS: THE CAMBRIDGE RING

The Cambridge Ring North East (Carnet) project was started by local residents in 1998 when they realized there was no prospect of either BT or cable companies providing broadband in the foreseeable future. The ring of villages around Cambridge has a high concentration of computer literate residents, many with University connections and others who work from home in related industries such as IT and graphic design. A few early adopters championed the cause, so sure where they that there would be sufficient take-up of broadband to defray the start-up costs. The supplier, Invisible Networks, is working with Carnet, a not-for-profit organization, and is bearing the capital cost of renting a leased line from Cambridge to the Bottisham telephone exchange and providing wireless antennae and receivers to connect local homes and businesses (Carnet, 2003).

Community uses of broadband are developing as the number of subscribers grows. One example of a much valued service is a webcam on the main commuter route into Cambridge, so that residents can plan their journeys to work.

The major advantage of broadband, however, is for those who are self-employed or work from home, and need to send and receive large files, images and diagrams. The increased speed now available through broadband has had a significant effect on the working practices of these people:

- Before broadband, information had to be sent on CDs through the post, or be broken up into smaller files to be sent individually.
- Working practices used to revolve around setting things running for several hours while other tasks were done.

- Access to clients' products used to be through printed brochures received by post. Now these products can be accessed online more readily and in a more up-to-date version.
- Before broadband, employees had to drive into the head office to pick up training material and large data files. These journeys are no longer necessary.

The conceptual barrier to working from home has really disappeared for these people. They produce work more quickly than before and can pace their work more appropriately.

COMPLEX DATA TRANSFERS: THE GREAT BOOK OF GAELIC

The example of An Leabhar Mor (the Great Book of Gaelic) illustrates some of the advantages of broadband for the transfer and access of complex digital data. This is a large, complex, and innovative cultural project that includes poetry, new artwork, a traveling art exhibition, a new glossy book (MacLean & Dorgan, 2002), Web site, educational pack for children, and a documentary film. Each aspect of the project has innovative and entrepreneurial elements, but for our current purposes we will focus on activities related to the Web site, though it is necessary to first describe the central concepts of the project.

The idea was conceived as an exploration of the cultural links between the Gaelic-speaking areas of Scotland and Ireland. A steering group and selection panel invited 15 Scottish and 15 Irish poets to nominate one of their own poems, and two others of their choice, with a further 10 poems nominated by a panel to give 100 poems in all, spanning writers from the 6th to the 21st centuries. One hundred visual artists were selected by nomination and open submission and then paired with a poem for which they then produced a creative response. Finally a team of calligraphers was selected to provide an additional response to the individual poems.

The interactive Web site(PNE, 2003) contains the text of the entire book with hypertext links, and thumbnail illustrations of all of the original works of visual art. Broader bandwidth is undoubtedly advantageous to view these complex illustrations speedily, but the real benefit of broadband access is realized by the next stage of project development. In this phase audio clips of each of the pieces of poetry are being added as hypertext links, combining digital sound with the literary and visual experience. Further plans for Web site development include invitations for new contemporary Gaelic poets to write their own interpretations of the visual art, and for new artists to respond in different ways to the poetry hosted on the site. In this way the site becomes both an archive of 'classical' culture, an organically growing vehicle for the contemporary expression of Scottish and Irish cultural links, and also a powerful teaching and learning resource.

HYPER-INTERACTIVITY: CROMARTY CONSULTANTS

Calico UK (2003) is an Internet service provider (ISP) and consultancy company that operates from a small fishing village on the north east coast of Scotland. The company was established in the early 1990s with the specific intention of bringing fast access Internet services to a wider range of small businesses and individual households in the Highlands and Islands of Scotland. To this end Calico UK was an early adopter of a dedicated fibre optic connection and though they work with large-scale corporate players, the majority of their clientele are small and micro businesses across the UK and specifically in this region. This has given them unrivaled access to customer and business intelligence on the requirements on the installation and use of telecommunications applications. After 7 years of broadband use they are established regionally, nationally, and internationally as a small and flexible group combining the ISP with communications consultancy and training.

They identify two strong elements in their successful adoption of extensive bandwidth in their business, the always-on property, and the fostering of trust between users of their online community. This includes a range of links and support for customers without broadband but who wish to adopt communications technology for their own purposes. Calico UK's use of broader bandwidth has resulted in changes to working practices that include a blurring of job demarcation in the company, and making use of the always-on property to share business information and workloads. Enquiries by email to the ISP helpline are posted to an internal staff conference where a number of staff are able to comment and respond with solutions. Other staff conferences are used to deal with work scheduling and specific tasks, as well as overtime and management records. Being pioneers in their area they were largely unable to utilize conventional training methods for staff, and have relied upon informal Web-learning and a high degree of knowledge-sharing, both between staff, and within a network of other companies. Online business relationships have frequently developed into reciprocal business relationships for their mutual benefit. The combination of ISP, training, and consultancy roles places Calico UK in a uniquely informed position to respond to a very varied network of customers and users, and to incorporate their use of broadband as a fixed asset of their business practice rather than simply a utility. They characterize the strengths of broadband in their business as "being able to find a good idea and share it with your colleagues" as well as "not just being what you bring to your online work, but also the added values to online and offline relationships."

ALWAYS ON: WELSH INTERNET RADIO

The example of Radio Acen (2003) demonstrates one of the advantages of the "always on" property of broadband by utilizing 802.11b technology (digital wireless) to operate a learning community, entertainment, and merchandising operation through the medium of Internet radio. In 2002 the Welsh National Assembly backed a community-based initiative called e-fro (2003) to demonstrate the value of 802.11b wireless technology, to stimulate the demand for broadband, and to create online communities to trial innovative projects in Wales (Welsh Assembly Government, 2003). After background research in the Ogwen Valley, west of Cardiff, into the potential links between broadband access and economic and cultural development, a number of pilot initiatives were tested, including wireless demonstrations at the Royal Welsh Show, the National Eisteddford, and a community links between Bangor and Bethesda.

From these initial trials grew a number of cultural and broadcasting initiatives, including the idea of a Welsh language Internet radio service, based upon a schedule of Welsh music with occasional topical prerecorded programs in Welsh. In effect, the radio service is offered as a soft "front" for both informal and structured opportunities to learn the Welsh language. A number of online courses in learning basic Welsh are available from the radio station home page, along with a selection of programs that can play on request. Listener feedback provides evidence of an international audience, with asynchronous access, largely among the diaspora of Welsh expatriates and their descendants. Online learning courses in this initial phase are being offered free, with the costs being recovered through online merchandising associated with the music and other cultural activities. The radio service was established as an entrepreneurial, private sector initiative, pooling the resources of a Welsh language development agency, TV broadcasting expertise, and a music recording company. The success of the venture is not only in capturing the interest of an international expatriate market, but in the ability to provide high quality digital sound reproduction on request, across time zones and times of day convenient to the users.

DISCUSSION

There are some fascinating insights to be observed in the treatment of the complex layers of connected technology, the human resources represented by the users of this technology, and the interaction between them. We have analyzed these processes as an example of a complex adaptive system, that we have labeled the Connecticon. It has some key emergent properties in common with other complex adaptive systems. The capacity for self organization is one such key component, and in fitting the parts together the Connecticon is shaped by elements of compatibility, convergence and convenience in terms of both the technological and human social systems. If machines are not able to speak to each other then the transmission of information is impaired, similarly the human contacts require a certain degree of trust and common interests in order to fruitfully exchange information, let alone achieve reciprocal benefit.

Stability domains in the Connecticon can be represented by the consolidation of the "background" of Internet traffic—the email—that is simple but effective and continues to grow despite the rise and wane of other "revolutionizing" technological innovations. It provides a steady state to balance the rapid leaps forward in other areas of the Connecticon. In both of these elements, however, the steady state and the radical change, there are startling new opportunities for new constructions of knowledge and increased understanding. A crucial factor in the communication of ideas is the ability for these ideas to replicate and therefore spread themselves throughout human society, and in this the first layer of the Connecticon, the infrastructure of the Internet, there is an excellent dispersal mechanism. From the entrepreneurial perspective, the creation and exploitation of new ideas, there is a dualism required in order to communicate high fidelity knowledge (e.g., shifting prices, or specific confidential information) together with the cultural transmission of knowledge (e.g., contextualizing and adapting) that need not be 100% accurate. A view of cultural evolution is becoming understood that treats the "self-replicating elements of culture passed on by imitation" as "units of information residing in a brain" and has labeled them "memes" by analogy to genes as the drivers of biological evolution. Looked at in this manner we can appreciate,

> that for cultural evolution to occur the fidelity of transmission must lie within a particular range. The fidelity cannot be 100% because culture would have no variation, which is required for differential survival to drive evolutionary change. The fidelity must still be very high, or else culture would have no continuity between individuals and "good tricks" would be lost as quickly as gained, and again evolution would not occur. (Rose, 1998)

The numerous changes to information that occur in its transmission around the Connecticon is another emergent property of the system—complex system cycles. It is supported by the actions of the second layer of the Connecticon, the human resource that interfaces with the technological infrastructure. The changes made by the human interface in amending, adapting, and contextualizing information occur both by accident and design, but do not occur with every communication of the information. It is this very mutation of an idea to create a slightly different meme that can be used to interpret progressive change of knowledge and understanding. Like its counterpart the gene, the meme does not control its own mutation, and with the infinitely large number of connections (possible and actual) and information is communicated across the super-network of the Connecticon, there are an infinite number of potential innovations will be created. These innovations may be copied and communicated to other parts of the system, but their persistence over time, like their counterparts in biological evolution, will depend upon natural selection of the ideas that are adapted to the environment that they reach. From the business or development perspective, the ideas that provide a useful function, whether it is a new source of profit, a more efficient way of operating, or a better organizational structure, will survive. If their survival persists, they may help to form a new domain of stability. If the mutation is only successful in the short-term, or the environment changes, then the meme will cease to be culturally appropriate, and like the collapse of dot.com companies, they will be replicated less frequently.

Most mutations are small scale, resulting in gradual evolution. Occasionally, an "entrepreneurial idea" comes along—a large scale mutation—and this results in a sudden and complete change of direction that changes the way people think and operate. In order to create an environment in which entrepreneurial ideas flourish, we need both the stable environment of progressive evolution as well as the openness to recognize the potential of novel ideas when they appear. The Connecticon is fundamental to understanding the survival of entrepreneurial ideas. The emergent properties of fast speed, complex data exchange throughout the network are matched by the properties of the human resource to provide the mutation and to interpret the good ideas. The mechanism for recognizing good ideas amongst the millions of mutations that provide no useful function is natural selection in a business context.

Part of the difficulty in recognizing and managing innovation in the Information Age is that information is not the only, or even the main economy that we are dealing with. It has been argued that we have too much information flowing around the system, and this superfluity has tended to lower the value of information while at the same time it has caused an increase in the value of attention (Goldhaber, 1997). As more demands are placed upon our attention, this becomes a more scare resource, spread more thinly to cope with the attention seeking demands of dealing with greater volumes of information. As we spend more effort on attention to information, we transform it into something that humans can use, and move with greater sophistication from 'raw data' through "useful information" to "wisdom" (Lankshear & Knoble, 2001). This reinforces the importance of the concept of the Connecticon as an interaction between the infrastructure of cyberspace and the human resource that uses investments in attention to sort out the overpowering flow of information into useable commodities (Lanham, 1994). A key feature in reading the emerging ecology of the Connecticon is the construction of filters and gateways that will allow the human users to "facilitate attention to information, to turn it into something useful for users and to enable users to use it more usefully in terms of their wants and goals" (Lankshear & Knoble, 2001). These intermediaries (filters, search engines, bots, etc.) will enable more meaningful use of collaborative online technologies, and in this respect "the 'virtual' is not the *opposite* of the 'real' it is a medial term, *between* the real and the artificial or imagined" (Burbules, 2001). They may assist us to envisage scenarios that can construct conventional data in new ways that can challenge our conventional predictions of the future, and the values or critical uncertainties that can be explored for new, innovative, and more appropriate solutions for future societies.

CONCLUSIONS

1. The complex merging of a networked technological infrastructure with the flexibility of the human resource of knowledge users and their opportunities for hyper-interactivity can be regarded as an example of a complex adaptive system that we have termed the Connecticon.

2. Key emergent properties of the Connecticon are exemplified by four of the key characteristics of broadband access to the Internet, namely (1) It enables information to be communicated many times faster than previously; (2) It allows transfer of more complex data sets; (3) It enables much greater interactivity between users (hyper-interactivity); and (4) It is always on and therefore truly global in its application.

3. Although our analysis of the Connecticon does not enable us to predict where or when innovation will occur, it suggests two conditions that will allow us to maximize the benefits of entrepreneurial activity: (1) the need to foster a culture of openness to new ideas, and (2) the need to support the emergent trends toward new ways of team working that include greater collaboration, transparency of knowledge communication, and multi-functional tasking.

Innovation, in business or in education is not something that can be taught, but clearly it can be learned.

CHAPTER 6

Learning with Learning Objects

LEARNING OBJECTS AND THE CONNECTICON

The explosion of information and what is more, readily available information on the Web, has fueled the concept of reuse of information in a range of different ways. In higher education, it may be a slight overstatement but more or less true, that when learners reuse information it is condemned as plagiarism but when course designers do it, it is hailed as re-versioning. Whatever it is called, we all reuse information, ideas and ways of expressing ideas in our work, our conversation and our

"This is the part I always hate."

Source: London Mathematical Society Newsletter. © Sidney Harris

writing. Of course there are conventions for acknowledging the origin of the words or ideas, but the notion of "origin" has already begun to be somewhat suspect and will be more so as the processes of the Connecticon continue to proliferate. The Internet is the focus of a massive tug-of-war—between those who want to make money from the Web as a multi-lane highway and those who enjoy the feeling of the open road. The former tries to impose the ownership rules of the paper world onto the vastly different cyber world; the latter have moved away from many of the strictures and conventions of the paper world and see the Web as a new playground with a different set of possibilities.

The collective attributes of the Connecticon are beginning to affect the traditional notions of ownership of information and ideas. Emerging from the information explosion, the rise in ubiquitous connectivity, and the Web as a vehicle for everyman to become a publisher, we are beginning to see a philosophical view of knowledge as a collective social product, something that should be openly available and owned collectively.

In education, the impact of so much readily available information is being felt across all roles and sectors. The changing role of the teacher in higher education has been well rehearsed. The changing role of the librarian has not been nearly so well acknowledged. Librarians are no longer simply custodians and cataloguers and the scope and magnitude of changes occurring in libraries are significant.

> The emergence of digital libraries and the widespread availability of electronic information have provided many opportunities to enhance the role of librarians in the information age in finding new ways to respond effectively and innovatively to a very different landscape in meeting user expectations. Today's librarians are taking responsibility in user education, knowledge management, organization of networked information resources, electronic publishing and curriculum development. (Duncan & Ekmekeioglu, 2003, p. 139)

Librarians will be key players in the reuse process in higher education.

THE LEARNING OBJECT RHETORIC

> The idea [of learning objects] is that you have a virtually instantaneous access to all possible learning and the way we do that is that we make it very easy to find learning and deliver learning. The way we make learning very easy to find is through the use of metadata. The way we make learning very easy to deliver is through our understanding of the pedagogy of learning objects. For example, we deliver in much smaller units of information than the typical class. We deliver five minutes of learning.... Now that is the theory. It turns out to be a lot harder than people first thought. There are significant issues—how do we meta tag? Who is going to do all that work? We need processes that allow as much of this meta tagging to be done automatically as possible. (Downes, 2003, pp. 164–165)

The rationale for reusing course material is that it should result in greater efficiency and higher quality. The smaller the item to be reused, the more feasible it is to use in a variety of teaching contexts—different levels, markets, curriculum areas. Hence the notion of a "learning object," a teaching resource which stands alone, i.e., does not depend on other objects to make sense. Governments around the world are investing significant sums of money in initiatives to develop large repositories of learning objects each of which is tagged with metadata to facilitate searching and storing. Both for K–12 teachers and for higher education, learning object repositories promise to provide high quality resources that can be easily identified, reused or re-versioned by teachers for their immediate application in the classroom or online course. Why create something yourself when someone else, probably more expert, has already done it? Why not share something you have created with others and reduce the reinventing of wheels? As teachers move away from being content producers and disseminators and move toward being facilitators of learning, reusing existing teaching material is an obvious step.

There is considerable variation in current perceptions about the size of a learning object (LO). For some stakeholders, an LO is what might be called a "lesson," and several lessons or LOs can be combined to form a module or a whole course. For others, an LO should be as small as possible—for example, a single screen may contain several LOs. Needless to say, a range of other terminology has arisen to cope with this difference in granularity:

- The notion of a "media object" has been used to refer to objects with video, audio or graphical elements.
- The term "interactive learning object" has been used to refer to simulations, games and diagrams with movable parts.
- Most significantly, many practitioners have drawn a distinction between "information objects" (sometimes known as "content objects") and "learning objects." This distinction separates mere facts from learning contexts within which facts are used.

Given so much variation about what actually constitutes an LO, it is surprising how much agreement there is about their attributes. They must be:

- Reusable—they can be modified and versioned for different courses;
- Accessible—they can be indexed for easy retrieval using metadata standards;
- Interoperable/portable—they can operate across different hardware and software irrespective of the original author;
- Durable—they can remain intact through upgrades to the hardware and software.

There is also considerable agreement about the need for LOs, revolving around the demand for lifelong learning that is timely, personalized and targeted. In particular, new learners are thought to want bite-sized chunks of learning, not whole courses. They want learning tailored to their individual context. They want flexibility of access and just-in-time content (Rehak & Mason, 2003, pp. 21–22).

Despite the interest and money being devoted to the concept of learning objects (admittedly most of this has been in the technical realization of the concept, not in the practical application), there has been little research into the pedagogical consequences of these systems and ways of thinking, and no examination of their epistemological and ideological implications (Friesen, 2004).

THE NOTION OF REUSE

There are numerous reuse scenarios conjured up by the learning object enthusiasts. In ascending order of likelihood, they are:

- The author of a learning object reuses the object on a different course.
- A colleague of the author in the same institution reuses the object in a different curriculum area.
- The author submits a number of learning objects to a national repository and in turn gets to use some created by others.
- A learner wants to create a course with a specific set of topics and pulls a range of learning objects from the repository for self-study.

While straight reuse of a learning object is one thing, re-versioning, editing, or altering the original is a different matter. Obviously the original becomes much more useful if it can be changed. If the changed version is added to the repository, it becomes even more useful. However, ownership and intellectual property (IPR) then become an issue. Three approaches are being discussed currently:

1. The Open Source approach, in which learning objects are openly available to all and re-versioning is encouraged with the proviso that the new version is added to the repository and can be further adapted by other users.
2. The closed club approach in which membership entitles participants to reuse and possibly adapt, assuming they contribute learning objects to the pool.
3. Commercial approaches in which users simply pay for what they reuse. Copyright rests with the original author, who usually does not permit adaptation.

Obviously the Open Source solution is most in keeping with libertarian views of the Internet, and with a global, one-world view of information. The decision by MIT to put its course content on the Web has given great impetus to this approach. Descriptions of other learning object repository applications follow.

Open Learning and the MIT Initiatives

MIT is currently engaged in two related projects: The Open Knowledge Initiative (OKI) and the Open CourseWare project (OCW). The aim of both is to assemble, deliver and make accessible Internet-based educational materials in learning object format. OKI provides an open source layered software architecture to host the OCW learning objects, which are freely available on the Web for noncommercial use.

The LMS that has been developed through OKI is called Stellar and consists of tools for uploading and organizing content, tools for access management and tools to support communication.

> By separating the presentation layer from the underlying software tools using XML and XLST, Stellar's look and feel are customizable. Faculty or departments can opt to have a particular graphic design for their Stellar class site, whether that means using particular terminology in a navigation bar, employing a certain colour set, or providing certain options such as anonymous feedback, embedded home page images, or a discussion board. . . . To aid faculty in repurposing content once it is online, Stellar contains a transfer tool that allows faculty to reuse pieces of content in other classes without having to upload them again. (Vale & Long, 2003, p. 62)

One of the ideas behind the Open CourseWare project was that developing countries could use the content to extend their curriculum, enhance the quality of existing courses and connect with "state of the art" teaching material. The extent to which this has actually been facilitated by OCW materials is somewhat confused. UNESCO sponsored a forum in July 2002 to bring together potential users to investigate the possibilities and difficulties of building on the OCW initiative. Representatives from universities in Mauritius, Guinea, Cameroon, Russia, Brazil, Egypt, Senegal and India attended. The problems of reuse that were raised by the delegates included:

- Translation—who would do it and who would pay for it; what about updates to the material; what about cultural as well as linguistic translation.

- Infrastructure requirements—equipment specifications, interoperability, standards, technical competencies of support staff, bandwidth.
- Institutional missions—local institutions and scholars need to be supported and not undercut by the provision of freely available courseware.

In short, while the concept of open courseware was acknowledged as timely and pertinent, it was obvious from the discussions that the availability of the content was only the very first of many problems to overcome in taking advantage of the initiative (UNESCO, 2002).

On the other hand, there is evidence of individual students and lecturers making good use of the OCW materials. A journalist for *Wired* magazine toured the globe exploring the use of the MIT materials and interviewing users from rural USA to Ho Chi Minh City in Vietnam.

One of the most popular offerings turned out to be Laboratory in Software Engineering, aka 6.170, a tough requirement for electrical engineering and computer science majors. Lam Vi Quoc, a fourth-year student at Vietnam's Natural Sciences University, relied on 6.170 lectures to supplement a software lab he was taking, and Evan Hoff, a software developer in Nashville, followed the course to improve his coding skills. In Karachi, Pakistan, a group of 100 students and professionals met weekly to study 6.170. In Kansas City, five members of the Greater Kansas City Java Professionals Association gathered monthly to take the course. In Mauritius, a tiny island nation in the Indian Ocean, Priya Durshini Thaunoo used 6.170 to prepare for a master's degree program at the University of Mauritius. Saman Zarandioon, an Iranian refugee living in Vienna, studied it to continue an education that was stalled by the Iranian government. And software developer Rahul Thadani in Birmingham, Alabama, took it to sharpen his skills. (Diamond, 2003)

It is interesting to note that when the material is simply made available openly, people use it; when institutions meet to consider it, all they see are insurmountable problems.

MERLOT

MERLOT is a collaborative effort of a consortium of higher education institutions. It is a free and open collection of learning objects designed for faculty and students of higher education. One feature of the MERLOT repository is the facility for adding annotations, peer reviews, comments and proposed assignments. Peer reviews are contributed by qualified faculty in the discipline(s) to which the material relates. Information about how others have used a particular learning object, or how they have designed an assessment to accompany it, obviously adds to its re-usability.

Another feature of this repository is that materials can be added by the people who created them, or by any member of the MERLOT organization (membership is free and open) who finds a resource they wish to share. When material is added by someone other than its author or creator, an email is sent to the person who owns it to let them know it has been listed in MERLOT.

In addition to the peer reviews of the learning objects commissioned from specially trained faculty, comments from any user are encouraged, much as they are on Amazon.com. The aim is to develop communities of practice which support faculty in choosing learning objects, customizing the material for their context, participating in professional development activities.

> There are a number of critical features to MERLOT that makes it more than a collection of urls. The individual members of MERLOT write descriptions of the materials within the context of teaching and learning. Members can add comments about the quality and use for the materials. MERLOT also provides the capability for members to describe specific techniques for using the materials in teaching; the Learning Assignments includes information about the topics covered, the level of student . . . , names of courses for which it is appropriate, pre-requisite skills and knowledge the students should have before doing the assignment, learning objectives, type of learning activity . . . , assessment methods, time required to do the assignment, and the text of the assignment. All the metadata on pedagogy enables faculty to effectively and easily choose and use the best online learning materials for their students that are compatible with their own teaching methods and the learning goals of their academic program. (Hanley, 2003, p. 4)

CLEO

The Co-operative Learnware Object Exchange is a collaborative project of eight Ontario universities to develop an innovative infrastructure for joint development of interactive learning resources. CLEO will increase access to learning opportunities by improving the return-on-investment for development through reuse of learnware objects, and accelerate the cultural change required for elearning to reach its potential in support of life-long learning. The key innovation in CLOE is the creation of a virtual market economy for engaging multimedia to support online learning. Each institution will develop multimedia learning resources to address instructional challenges shared by the other partners. Each institution will contribute educational multimedia to the co-operative exchange and use resources developed by the other institutions in return. The virtual market will encourage collaboration across institutions to pool ideas and co-ordinate development: the most successful resources—those reused the most—will provide the most exchange credit for the institutions developing them. Resources only used by the original developers will not accrue exchange credits, so a substantial incentive for collaboration is built into CLOE.

The major innovation in CLOE is the co-operative exchange mechanism. The motivation for the co-operative exchange is threefold:

- Increase elearning opportunities, by making high quality resources more widely available.
- Increase the return on investment for development of learning resources, by compensating institutions whose resources by used by others. This also promotes high quality in the resources, since learnware objects which are reused by others return more value.
- Accelerate the growth of effective communities of practice for elearning development. In keeping with the university cultures, these will be discipline-based. We are already experimenting with support for such communities in early stage design reviews, to insure that resources can be more easily reused and to build "buy-in" for reuse (Carey, 2001).

The CLEO consortium is working with MERLOT staff to understand the issues of sharing and sustainability. Unlike the MIT OCW approach in which one institution provides and all the others are merely users, CLEO is developing a cooperative exchange in which everyone is both producer and consumer.

> The idea is not to enforce the exchange mechanism so that if you are out of credits, you cannot get to use any of the objects. The idea is to ensure that people investing in those objects are considering who else might use them. The way to ensure reuse and hence a much large benefit, is to have some mechanism to capture and document those benefits so that all the institutions find it in their best interest to make investments collaboratively. (Carey, 2003, p. 116)

This is a refinement of the babysitting co-op.

Candle

A European initiative, called Candle, has been instigated by the EUNICE network, a European network of telematics education, to encourage and promote an exchange of learning resources to improve quality and efficiency within education. This is a research and development project funded by the European Commission as part of its Fifth Framework Programme.

The aim is to establish an information brokerage system that will support the exchange of course materials across an international network of institutions. The second goal is to provide a set of reusable resources and to evaluate their reusability within the Europe-wide testbed. The third goal is to develop and evaluate a methodology to enable instructors to improve the reusability of their own resources (Wetterling & Collis, 2003, p. 183).

Unlike the other initiatives described here, Candle is much more than a repository of learning objects (and in many ways much less than a repository). It is trying to establish a learning object economy:

- Authors collaboratively designing and developing shareable, reusable course material;
- Instructors sharing course material and exchanging their experiences of reuse;
- Learners from a single course working together across cities, countries and even continents.

At the moment, most learning object repositories are free to users. It is debatable whether commercial versions will ever become viable. On the other hand, are freely available materials going to be sustainable, once initial funding runs out and enthusiasm of authors' wanes? When IPR prevents change and adaptation, it is hard to see that users will find "fixed" learning objects suitable enough, often enough to make commercial systems workable. One of the earliest pioneers in the use of learning objects, David Wiley, notes:

> The commercial content industries have learned the hard way that, despite rights management attempts, digital content will make its way into free distribution. This fact of Internet life will prevent an "educational object economy" in which large amounts of commercial content are available for purchase and reuse from ever materializing. (Wiley, 2003)

While the notion of learning objects is still very much in the early stages of development, the cynics have noted that while there may be some providers, there are few users (i.e., reusers), even of free repository objects.

IMPLEMENTING REUSE

In many ways the term "learning object" encapsulates the dichotomy at the heart of reuse. The choice of the word "object" has clear origins in object oriented programming. The form of design and analysis used in object oriented programming has had a strong influence in the groups that are responsible for the technical standards being developed to support learning objects. Learning, on the other hand, has no such all-pervasive approach and the underlying paradigm fluctuates, if indeed it could be said that such an ill-structured domain as learning has an underlying paradigm.

> It is at this point that it becomes possible to understand why the term "learning object" has been the cause of such controversy. The term "learning object" juxtaposes two words that are in many ways incongruous and ultimately, incommensurable: The first, "object: is a thoroughly and very specific technological paradigm. . . . It is part of an approach whose basic principles are so specialized as to be difficult to express in everyday language. And the second, "learning" is equally extreme in its vagueness, generality and broadly non-technical nature. In clear contrast to the dominance of the object-oriented paradigm in programming and software design, there is no consensus among educational experts as to how learning occurs or how it can best be understood. (Friesen, 2004, p. 61)

This dichotomy continues in the principle concerns of different users of learning objects. Those who are interested in reuse and repurposing of learning materials see the advantages of learning objects as part of the change process in higher education—moving away from teaching as being about content toward seeing learning as a process which teachers need to facilitate and support. The President of Athabasca, Canada's main distance teaching university notes:

> Ten years from now—five years from now perhaps—Athabasca won't be developing content in the same way as it does today. Today, we develop primarily our own content, but, if you're going to develop it for the multimedia environment, it is far too expensive for an institution to do that. Even if you enrol 100 to 200 students in your course, it is just not an economically feasible model. Commercial publishers will develop multimedia learning activities to support the sale of their textbooks. . . . They can develop quality materials that we could not even start to develop at the institutional level. In the next five to seven years, a place like Athabasca is going to have to shift its way of developing content and to become much more an institution that is going to restructure content that will be multimedia that will actually be developed by others. (Abrioux, 2003, pp. 16–17)

Another set of interests focuses around the notion—the aim—of learners or learning providers being able to assemble a course "on the fly" from a large repository of objects. Aggregating content in this way is more appropriate in training, where it is effective for teaching rudimentary skills or for competency or performance-based subjects, where the emphasis is on what people want or need to know, not on what there is to be known.

The implementation problems for this latter group center around the tagging, storing and retrieving of learning objects, and there is a voluminous literature expounding these issues (see, e.g., McGreal, 2004; Little-john, 2003; Wiley, 2003). For the former, the implementation issues are largely pedagogical and cultural. Problems of sharing and reuse arise between institutions which all tend to have different instructional strate-gies, vocabularies, preferred topics and credit systems. Furthermore, teach-ers whether in campus settings using lectures or in distance education using tailor-made print materials, are used to integrating instructions, objectives, and references forward and backward in the course material. In short, they view the course as one indivisible chunk. Separating out these process elements from the content elements is the first priority in working in learning objects.

> A common problem with conventional materials is that the instruction is inextricably linked with the resources and it is very difficult to separate them out. When the various items are not designed and developed discretely, they can really only be used in the precise setting for which they have been built. (Oliver & McLoughlin, 2003, p. 100)

Cultural issues begin with the problem of resistance amongst some aca-demics to sharing their materials at all and particularly to using material developed by others. In short, they have no incentive to participate in the learning object economy. Others object to the whole concept of "chunk-ing" learning into small bites, seeing this as trivializing and commodifying learning and losing the narrative flow which at the heart of the difference between knowledge and information.

CREATING COURSES FROM LEARNING OBJECTS

While it is easy to see how teachers can incorporate learning objects into their course, whether it is lecture-based or print-based, it is somewhat more challenging to design a course entirely from learning objects. The reason is alluded to in the description above of the traditional course in which con-tent, resources, instructions, activities, testing and even personal comments and anecdotes are woven into one inextricable whole. Using some learning objects in an otherwise traditional course does not disturb this integrated process as the new material is essentially another resource on the course. However, how does this integrating function take place when the whole course consists entirely of discrete objects which do not refer to each other? Where is the "glue" that holds the course together and provides the value-added difference from self study or browsing in a library?

Various approaches to designing whole courses from learning objects are being tried by the enthusiasts. The one described here is based on the idea of the learning object as microcosm, somewhat akin to a lesson. Rather than defining a learning object as the smallest discrete item of material and aggregating many of them to make up a topic, the opposite tack is taken. The learning object is conceived as a summation or expert overview of a topic, consisting of explanatory text, selected reading resources and follow up material, and activities in which the learner can engage experientially with the subject. Each learning object might involve anywhere from one to five hours of work on the part of the learner. The objects are all stand alone, discrete learning opportunities, which the learner might hope to complete in one study session. Collaborative working possibilities are included in many of the activities which assume a synchronous or asynchronous discussion area associated with the objects. Other activities might involve simulations, spreadsheet manipulations, or various forms of interactive elements. The essence of the approach is that the learning object is a holistic experience for the learner: exposition, interaction, engagement, and feedback all within a student-directed learning environment offering choice and flexibility for learners to investigate the topic in their own way. The "glue" is supplied in one non-reusable learning object at the beginning of each week's work. This sets out the aims, highlights recurring themes, makes suggestions about how to tackle the work, and so on.

This level of granularity for learning objects circumvents many of the problems others have experienced with smaller chunks of learning, and provides something of a solution to the "loss of narrative" and decontextualisation objections. In fact, there is some evidence that this larger granularity is being adopted by others in higher education. Certainly it has proved a successful and popular approach on one course (see, Mason, Pegler, & Weller, 2004).

An approach to the problems associated with using learning objects constructed by someone else is that instead of reusing content, we should be reusing frameworks, templates and software. In fact the holistic approach to learning object design described here is an example of a framework that could be applied to many different curriculum areas.

Wiley claims:

> LOs should not contain content at all; rather they should contain the educational equivalent of algorithms—instructional strategies (teaching techniques) for operating on separately available, structured content. (Wiley, 2003)

Another example would be a database of generic learning activities which course designers could use to get ideas to apply to their own curriculum area. The notion of reusing frameworks rather than content would go some way to addressing the pedagogical and cultural problems outlined throughout the chapter.

Polsani (2003) examines the relationship between learning objects and electronic books. He concludes that content is important but sees learning objects as liberating learning from the tyranny of textualization:

> LOs that are appropriately conceived and constructed will be the first build-ing blocks for rapidly and efficiently constructing targeted reader experi-ences. LOs can play an important role, especially in etextbooks and learning materials since knowledge organized into reusable LOs can be easily com-bined to produce educational materials. However, I would like to emphasize that we should strive to move beyond the text-centric approach and concen-trate on designing participatory environments that engender memorable experiences in readers and audiences. (Polsani, 2003)

EXAMPLES OF LEARNING OBJECTS

A range of different kinds of learning objects are demonstrated, although of course print is not the right medium to give more than a taste of what these materials are like to view online, or to use in teaching and learning. Nevertheless, they give some idea of the range of possibilities. Four types are exemplified:

1. LO as small component of a Web page
2. LO as a lesson
3. Interactive LO
4. Multimedia LO

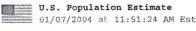

U.S. Population Estimate 01/07/2004 at 11:51:24 AM Est	**World Population Estimate** 01/07/2004 at 16:51:24 GMT(EST+5)
292,330,815	**6,340,728,964**
Source: U.S. Census Bureau, Population Division	Source: U.S. Census Bureau, International Programs Ctr.
U.S. POPClock notes	World POPClock notes
NOTE: The U.S. POPClock has been recalibrated to be consistent with Census 2000 data released on 12/28/2000	

Figure 6.1.   Population clocks http://www.census.gov/main/www/popclock.html

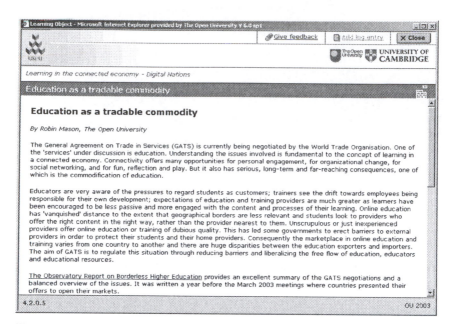

Figure 6.2.   Extract from the learning object on the GATS talks from Learning in the Connected Economy, a course on the Masters in Online and Distance Education *http://iet.open.ac.uk/coursesonline/ode/index.cfm*

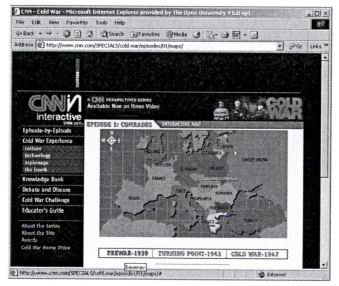

Figure 6.3.   *http://www.cnn.com/SPECIALS/cold.war/kbank/maps/*
Note: This screen shot is taken from CNN Interactive collection of maps of the Cold War. The map changes to show the effects of the Cold War at different points in history.

Figure 6.4.   Clip from the Multimedia Learning Object developed by Cambridge University for Learning in the Connected Economy.

CONCLUSION

We have examined the way in which the fascination with learning objects reflects aspects of the Connecticon: the re-use of learning resources, the notions of open content, the lure of greater efficiency and the opportunity to develop learner-centered materials that fit student study habits.

We have also considered the pedagogical concerns about the loss of narrative, and the trivialization of learning. Issues of ownership and commercialization of information have also been raised.

Several instances of learning object repositories have been described and issues of re-use explored. One approach to the granularity problem of learning objects has been proposed, based on holistic approaches to teaching.

CHAPTER 7

Pervasive Learning

INTRODUCTION

Consider the following scenario. When Fiona wakes in the morning she is still thinking about something she read in an ebook the following evening before she went to bed. As a result, immediately after breakfast she goes on to her home

E-MAIL, VOICE MAIL, CELL PHONE, BEEPER, FAX MACHINE, PDA... SO MANY GREAT NEW WAYS TO IGNORE PEOPLE!

GLASBERGEN

Source: Randy Glasbergen at: http://www.glasbergen.com/cat.html

computer and posts a question on the discussion board of an online learning study course that she is taking as a part of her continuous professional development at her workplace. Being late, she then has to dash to catch the commuter train to work. On the train while reading notes for a meeting later that day, she receives a text message on her mobile phone, a reply to her message on the discussion board from a fellow student that has been relayed to her mobile. The message gives a short comment on her question and suggests a URL where she can find more resources. Fiona scans the recommended website on her wireless laptop and locates a journal article that is highly relevant to the subject of her afternoon meeting with business clients. She forwards the URL of the article to a work colleague in the main office and also clicks to print a paper copy that she can collect from her own office and read at leisure. When Fiona leaves the train she continues on to the destination of her morning meetings. During the morning Fiona's colleague receives the journal article and is stimulated by its contents to add some text and digital photographs to better explain the context of a keynote presentation for the afternoon meeting. He passes it onto a third colleague who adds some diagrams, links it to a slide presentation, and uploads it to the company intranet site for group consideration. When Fiona arrives at the location of her afternoon meeting, her laptop automatically downloads the newest version of the discussion document and slide presentation for display on the walls of the boardroom. The committee members who live in other regions and are not able to be present in person have linked via videoconference and are able to receive copies of all the presentation materials at the same time as their colleagues, enabling a full and candid discussion to take place.

There are several important characteristics of this scenario that are worth noting. First, this is not science fiction, it is science-factual. These technologies for network communication and learning already exist, though their uptake is globally limited due to limited network coverage, technological costs and training, and the inertia of changing the culture of working practices. Second, the scenario describes the process of blended learning, a concept with which we are all familiar (although we usually do not dignify it with its own title) and which we will discuss in more detail later in this chapter. Third, the scenario underlines the growing importance of mobile access to information and communications networks, and indirectly the increasingly flexibility for learning and working that mobile access enables. Fiona was able to interact with resources at home, on the train, in her own office, and the offices of her clients; she was able to enlist the support of fellow students/tutors, work colleagues on multiple sites, and engage the participation of customers/employers with both synchronous and asynchronous interaction. Lastly, the scenario indicates the narrowing (possibly removal) of the divide between work-based activities and learning activities. The recognition of opportunities for situated learning, and the growing ability to access learning resources almost anywhere at almost any time have given strength to the concept of pervasive learning.

We should perhaps explain what we mean by "pervasive learning."

Embedded in the idea of pervasive services infrastructure (Milojicic et al., 2002), and sometimes colloquially expressed as "together whenever" the concept of a network of different devices that can "understand" each other, is combined with mobile access (and therefore situation-based connectivity) to give always-on opportunities. Some people may be horrified by this apparent inability to escape from the presence of technological connectivity, the feeling that they are always "on duty" of simply "being watched," but let's look at the learning implications. To us, pervasive learning is characterized by three key features, (1) the opportunities and affordances of blended learning; (2) the opportunities of mobile connectivity (or at least connectivity on the move, which may not quite be the same thing); and (3) the convergence of learning opportunities that are situated in the workplace, a domestic setting, or indeed in society at large. It is useful to explore and clarify these characteristics in some detail.

BLENDED LEARNING

This has become somewhat of a buzzword in educational circles, and like its counterpart "sustainability" the term has come to be an icon that means almost anything to anybody. We have a more structured understanding. Blended learning per se is not new, we can all realize that people learn in many different ways, sometimes from books, or scientific articles in journals, sometimes from the television or radio, frequently from friends and colleagues, or from complete strangers that we never meet again. Some of this learning is formal, much of it is informal, and it stands to reason that if we can somehow create the optimal mix of learning for an individual—both the content and the method of their engagement with learning—then we can harness both the motivation and the opportunity for continuous learning. Our definition of blended learning is a customized mix of these learning opportunities that takes cognition of the subject(s) being learned, the level of study, the method of interaction with the tutor (and other learners), as well as the abilities and motivations of the learner. So blended learning is not new, but there are two aspects that give it a new and more important resonance for education, work, and wider society. First, as Clark has argued,

> The fact that we have so many options [for learning] has forced us into thinking about how we can methodically choose an optimal mix. (Clark, 2003b, p. 7)

Second, the variety and complexity of the Connecticon have enabled us to recognize a complex ecology of learning that not only presents new sources of information, the basic building blocks of knowledge, but because this ecosystem is networked, allows us to share it collaboratively in almost limitless combinations.

So what are these components of blended learning that we need to structure carefully for optimal effect? Many of them you will already know. Printed materials such as books, journals, magazines, newspapers, and manuals are traditional source materials for learning, and of course all of these have their "modern" counterpart online—Virtual Learning Environments (VLE), online journals, and published websites. A halfway house provides offline digital versions of the printed materials through audio or video tapes, CD, DVD and videotapes. Another part of the blend is face-to-face tuition, as either a large class in the lecture theater, a small tutorial group dealing with particular topics, or one-to-one tuition on personal work. Again, all of these also have online equivalents in online conferencing, module discussion boards, videoconferences, email, and telephone connections, both group and individual. We could consider a sliding scale of complexity from email (one-to-one or one-to-small groups) through online discussion boards (interactive conversations between small and medium groups—large groups can be catered for by a hierarchy of links discussion boards or conferences) to "virtual" learning environments and online classrooms (integrated resources and collaborative networks). We use the term "virtual" in parenthesis because we believe that these learning environments are not virtual, they are real, with real students and real interaction, albeit of a newer form (or different blend). The growth of distance and "open" learning saw the development of educational materials broadcast on radio and television—frequently at off-peak hours early in the morning and later at night—and again these have evolved online equivalents. Keynote lectures can be captured as webcasts or recorded for Internet radio transmission on demand, and technical activities such as medical operations, interview techniques, and seminar discussions can be asynchronously available to students when required. Although interactive television is also developing to provide an element of asynchronicity, we have yet to see the full convergence with Internet resources that would allow seamless click-button access to archived TV programs, linked educational resources, that allows learners to navigate through their own educational needs. With the steady growth of communications protocols that enable the infrastructural components of the Connecticon to exchange information, we can expect the current generation of computers, laptops, PDA's, and mobile phones to be augmented by smart chips that encourage mobile real-time video connections, automatically updated diaries, access to vastly greater searchable repositories of information and knowledge, and smart technologies that at present we don't even fantasize clearly about. Here it is important to reintroduce a key distinction between information (data) as opposed to knowledge (how we use data) and the end-goal of understanding (the ability to manage and recombine knowledge for desired purposes). The goal of learning is ultimately to understand a subject, and so blended learning becomes recognized as a set of tools for knowledge management that we can exploit in different combinations that are relevant to the nature of the problem, the context, and the learner.

Notwithstanding the large numbers of people who take part in formal courses of learning, there are two innate situations in which learning takes place—the workplace, and in our recreational time. The challenge of life-long learning is to merge these social areas—the classroom, the workplace, and the recreational areas of our lives in a structured manner that enables us to continually relearn how to learn, i.e., to improve our knowledge management skills for the changing situations of our lives.

Consider this next scenario. Catriona is working from home to prepare a report for her job with a local authority. She is able to work quickly and efficiently using her broadband Internet connection to collect large files from colleagues in other offices and edit the results together for further sharing. By midmorning she has made fast progress but is unsettled, the weather outside is bright and breezy after weeks of rain and she would rather go outside even if it means finishing the report in the evening. She takes a look at a webcam of a local beach and sees with delight that the sea is perfect for a bit of wind surfing. Catriona switches the webcam to the URL that gives her password-protected access to her child's nursery school where she is able to see her daughter playing happily with the other children. Thus reassured Catriona sends an instant message to her three co-workers suggesting that they meet up for some surfing. Seconds later two of them reply positively and the third person, Quentin, dials up for a short video connection to discuss the project with Catriona. As a result of the conversation Quentin, who is just back from holiday, agrees to compile the completed pieces of the report and to add some resources to the webliography to strengthen the report's proposals. Catriona emails her part of the report and departs for a few hours surfing.

After the water sports Catriona and her colleagues drop into a local restaurant for a late lunch and take the opportunity to discuss their project. There is only a little bit to complete on the project and they divide the work up accordingly. Lydia, a junior member of the team, agrees to prepare an interactive database to collect and analyze responses to the report from councillors and senior officials. She sees a way that she can count the work toward part of her continuous professional development. Agnes also sees a way that she can benefit. She is completing a course in professional management and she will be able to explain the group thinking as part of the activities for two or three learning objects of her course. She agrees to review the project methodology and results on her departmental weblog later that day. As they finish their meal they exchange text messages with Quentin on the progress of the report then depart their own ways. In the evening, after the children are in bed, Catriona downloads the completed report and associated papers and burns a master CD of the project for copy and distribution to councillors and senior officials the next day.

This example is simply indicative. You can choose your own priorities and replace the media of learning connectivity with one that makes more sense to you. In fact, that is exactly the point! The fact is that all learners select their own blend, often by default in response to their learning motivation, and this blend frequently crosses back and forth between "formal" and "informal" learning styles. It is precisely this auto-selection that has produced the enormous rise in "open" learning over "traditional" (i.e., classroom-based) learning, with students voting with their feet (and their checkbooks) for more flexible styles of tuition and learning that accord more appropriately with their own lifestyles and motivations for learning. In time, the explosion of online learning opportunities that are currently appearing throughout the Connecticon will settle down, to present a number of sustainable models that harness the optimal advantages of the components of the blend according to the subject matter, academic level, and the learning objectives of the learner. If big, conservative universities do not listen to their learners and move to share their resources—albeit striving to excel in their own specialist areas—then students will bypass them to seek institutions that will. Is it any surprise?

Both of us have facilitated conferences and seminars in which we have tried to maximize the opportunities for informal learning, for example in small interactive workshops, side-meetings, or over drinks or a meal. We have purposefully encouraged this, even at the expense of "formal" learning events such as keynote speakers and plenary papers (despite the fact that many academics only get their expenses paid if they are delivering a paper!) and the results have often been startling. The opportunities to interact and engage with learning is a direct stimulant that encourages greater participant motivation. The trick, of course, is to match the optimal blend of learning styles and resources so that the learners are able to access structured learning experiences, not simply randomized hit-and-miss chunks of unrelated knowledge. This is where the ecology of the Connecticon is able to excel. The combination of multiple platforms for communications and data access, together with networked hyper-interactivity that supports an almost infinite pool of human resources (network users) can enable sensitively customized pathways of learning.

Like all new technology, however, there are down sides as well as benefits. In order to limit chronic information overload, pick-and-mix learning objects, and inappropriate or unreliable learning pathways, there needs to be opportunities for careful guidance and thoughtfully structured varieties of blended models. In order to utilize the Connecticon for learning, there needs to be a reliable mechanism for the recognition, selection, retention, and application of knowledge in a variety of different contexts relevant to the components of the Connecticon ecology. Clark (2003b) identified four principle types of blend, and Harrison (2003) suggested a process for constructing the optimal blend for any individual learning program. Their four types of blend comprise,

1. A Component blend—which essentially "bolts together" stand-alone learning resources (perhaps a lecture series plus a textbook plus a number of tutorials). Different courses may lay different emphasis upon whether or not the components require to be undertaken in a specific order.

2. The Integrated blend—is designed to "knit together" the learning resources in such a way that they are mutually supporting and inter-related, with specific crossovers identified between resources.

3. A Collaborative blend—reinforces the extent of resource integration by including the element of collaborative interactivity into the learning experience. Collaboration (face-to-face or online) between Tutor and learner and also learner-to-learner entails a two-way exchange of knowledge between participants and lifts the blend beyond the simple "delivery" of the first two blended models.

4. The Expansive blend—they argue, introduces the wider, less predictable use of learning resources by the learners and consequently moves beyond the formal learning resources supplied by the course designer to include a varied range of non-formal learning resources.

We find this latter model of blended learning particularly interesting and relevant for individualized learning in a hyper-connected society, and we will explore the significance of informal learning in more detail in the next chapter. Although the vastly increased scope and scale of accessible learning sources that are available for the construction of blended learning models are a major new factor influencing the rise of pervasive learning, it by no means the only factor. The ability of students to select not only the types of learning resources, but when and how they are able to access them in a manner compatible with the learners own lifestyle and motivational choices, is affected strongly by innovations in how mobile technology is able to interact within the ecology of the Connecticon.

MOBILITY IN THE CONNECTICON

Key features of the emerging ecology of the Connecticon are:

1. The multiple types of access employed by individual users,
2. The inter-connectivity of digital information.
3. The unpredictability of the exploitation of the user interface.

The growth in popularity of home Internet access, personal mobile phones, laptop/palmtop computers and other devices, e.g., GPS technology has provided a rich interactive environment for one-to-many communication and exchange of information. It is not the intention here to review the growth and impact of recent mobile access to networking technologies, this has been more than adequately covered by publications such as Rheingold's (2002) "Smart Mobs." The key factor for us is that mobile access to computer networks enables society to realize new possibilities for learning opportunities that pervade our day-to-day life. In particular, mobile learning can be enhanced in four ways.

First, the ease of transfer of digital information means that there can be enhanced interconnectivity between the software and hardware used to support individual communications. There can be continuum of connectivity between multiple types of access (PC, video-link, mobile phone, pager) and learning resources (word processed files, graphics, audio/video clips, live person-to-person connections) that can be flexibly adapted to suit the learner on the move. Although next generation devices incorporate new means of communications (e.g., mobile phones that have a built-in digital camera and email, or video-streaming capabilities) major challenges remain to ensure that (a) the new capabilities are compatible with the developing market; and (b) that there can be a seamless transition from one device to another (e.g., starting a business meeting via videoconference at work, continuing the discussion via hands-free mobile in the car, and rejoining the meeting in audio and video on the desktop PC at home). "The premise of pervasive (or ubiquitous) computing is that it should become invisible, threaded into the lives of users" (Milojicic, 2002, p. 3).

Second, the many-to-many lines of communication allow an almost continual access to information that the second layer of the Connecticon (the individual user) can utilize and (re)interpret. This has highly significant implications not simply for what information is used (and reused) to be converted (re-mixed) into knowledge and understanding (ideas and innovations) but also is a key driver in the development of appropriate technology itself. The case of the spread of text messaging is now a classic example. Despite the development of technically superior, high-fidelity mobile phones with Internet access, the public failed to get enthusiastic about them and instead enthusiastically adopted the "cheap and cheerful" alternative of text messaging that has circled the planet in epidemic proportions. This aspect—the self-organisation of users and the consequential emergence of unpredictable new properties and trends is a distinguishing feature of complex adaptive systems. In the Connecticon, each layer (infrastructure, human users, hyper-interaction) has self-organisation as a fundamental emergent property, with the result that the combination at the level of the complete system (the Connecticon) encourages flexibility, rapid evolutionary progression, and a volatility that is both positive (rapid spread of new ideas and innovation) and negative (rapid spread of viruses and collapse of dot.com companies). Although we will not go into it here, it is important to appreciate that we are speaking of "progress" according to the definition of Blackmore, not in the sense of progress toward a particular goal or objective, but:

> only increasing design, increasing complexity, or any kind of continuous development without a particular goal or end point built in. . . . there is no progress toward some predetermined or ultimate goal. (Blackmore, 2000, p. 28

Third, the ability to embed information (including different, alternative, sometimes contradictory types) in real objects (e.g., works of art, direction signs, tourist guides), permits users to consult, select, and re-use vast archives of information according to the particular context. We are really only at the very beginning of pervasive learning systems that allow users on the move the flexibility of location-aware access (Kindberg et al., 2003), but the ability to access, at will, interrelated layers of information that are located in the Connecticon (e.g., on the Web) but that are also rooted to physical objects in the real world, offers exciting and strange (sometimes scarily futuristic) visions of learning in the second half of the 21st century.

A fourth way in which mobile learning can enhance the learner experience (and usefulness) is in the interactive nature of computer processing power that enables the scrutiny of powerful background resources. These may include relational databases (phone/address lists, marketing information, government statistics, data storage) and computational functions (predictive financial scenarios, engineering models, software programming solutions) that enable the learner on the move to construct, deconstruct, and reconstruct different simulations or scenarios that can contribute to their understanding and/or alter their subsequent patterns of behavior. Combined with simultaneous access to peer-to-peer communications and a collaborative learning culture, these are extremely powerful learning tools. Again, a key factor here is that the user drives the learning process by the services that they demand and the manner in which they can interact with the resources.

In reality, of course, these four factors are interrelated and may be operationally inseparable. The reality of always-on, multi-platform connectivity for learning is so relatively new, (and still so geographically limited) that there are few realistic examples that could have mass application. Those that are available (e.g., Coatta, 2002) highlight the fact that learning happens at different times and in different contexts, so technologies that enable the seamless transition between the locations of the learner and focus with more relevance on the context of the learning situation, will become more important in a fast-changing and mobile society. An example might be the use of mobile phones (voice or text messaging) to provide a traveling business person with live-time language translation of keywords, or the use of hand-held web-surfing devices to download factual information in a range of languages about local statues, galleries/museums, or other sites of interest that have been "web-enabled" (Kindberg et al., 2003). The possibilities of different universities, schools, and public arts institutions creating their own networks of object-embedded course information for their own students offers tantalizing potential for both the sharing (and joint development) of learning resources between educational institutions (Mason, 1998) and also the structured merging of non-formal and formal learning for the lifelong learner.

Most significantly this raises not only the issue of multitasking but returns us to the situated learning of the complex adaptive system. From the perspective of analyzing multilingualism in a pervasive learning environment, Visser argues that,

> It is not difficult to see the above characteristics [of complex adaptive systems] represented in both living organisms, such as humans, and the larger systems with which they interact. Learning is an important dimension of the process through which humans stay in tune with their human, biological, and physical environment and through which that environment is allowed to take shape around them. (Visser, 1997, p. 2)

He further speculates that "... learning is an optional faculty, given to organisms by nature, that allows them to cope with unpredictability in their environment" (Visser, 1997, p. 2). In other words it allows humans to be flexible in their ability to learn and to innovate.

The significance of the Connecticon as a complex adaptive system for learning is therefore incalculably large. The restructuring of learning opportunities and resources through pervasive communications systems in the Connecticon constitutes an interactive construction that allows us to continually reposition ourselves with respect to the global ecosystem (and the tiny portion of it that we usually occupy). In previous decades learning was in general much more localized, both in terms of the blend that was available to learners ("take it or leave it—survival of the fittest" learning) and in terms of the impact that one individual could have on another (e.g., in the "cascading" of knowledge from expert to peers or pupils). However the learning possibilities resulting from the emergent properties of the complex adaptive system we are calling the Connecticon (like all complex adaptive systems) creates new levels of social interaction, and new levels of complexity of emergent properties at the different levels of engagement for the individual, small groups, communities, and the global population.

Even without the innovative possibilities resulting from greater access to structured assemblages of digital learning objects and the blurring of the divide between formal and non-formal learning events, there is a fundamental change of perspective that Visser notes "puts the emphasis on learning—what you do to yourself with others—rather than on education—what is being done to you" (Visser, 1997, p. 4). There is also a corresponding and more subtle shift directed toward reinforcing the internal motivation of self-directed learners, a shift that is further strengthened through engagement with pervasive learning techniques and informal learning resources that are available on a distributed basis.

Brown explored this web-based landscape of distributive learning properties to:

> see how they might create a new kind of information fabric in which learning, working, and playing co-mingle [and] examine the notion of distributed intelligence. (Brown, 2000, p. 12)

As we have said before, the benefits of new technologies do not come without a potential downside, and many of us may shrink today from the notion of "always-on" connectivity and learning that pervades every aspect of our lives. We believe that this is simply a transient phase. The deeper penetration of online access for distributed learning networks, peer-to-peer communications for learning and for leisure, that challenge traditional geographical and sectoral constraints (e.g., mobile ICT, wireless networks, smart networking solutions) are creating a new form of literacy. Although higher education has apparently made a greater effort to capture the benefits (to students and tutors) of online learning, it has shied away from extending its resources to provide seamless links with informal and experience-based learning that is appropriate for the new situations of learners. Brown emphasized the various ways in which we learn from each other, and in particular the way in which:

> learning becomes situated in action; it becomes as much social as cognitive, it is concrete rather than abstract, and it becomes intertwined with judgement and exploration. (Brown, 2000, p. 14)

The ability of the infrastructural layer of the Connecticon to pervade our entire personal world, whether in the workplace, at home, in the leisure center, the shopping mall or on the move, enables us to base our learning in the real situations of our world—not compartmentalized artificially. In this context entrepreneurial learning becomes learning that occurs on the node where two or more communities of practice (Connecticon spaces) interact or overlap. The juxtaposition of two or more new ideas, filtered and interpreted by the user in the light of their own experiences and abilities becomes the spark of entrepreneurialism, created in part by the navigational skills and partly by the coalescence of experience that the user brings to the situation. The ideas, once mixed, become part of a narrative that is retold to other members of the community, in different ways for different contexts, and in this way we continue the loop of being both the creators and consumers of our own knowledge. The operation of the Connecticon, to support relationships between people and to access vast repositories of cross-cultural information and knowledge, both creates and maintains the flexibility of our human role as simultaneous creators and consumers of knowledge. In this scenario, social capital becomes an outcome of interaction and participation in networks, rather than just a process (Simpson et al., 2003, p. 115). Whether it is on-the-job vocational training, corporate elearning networks, or informal learning situations such as peer referral on Amazon and eBay, the greatest challenge that we face is to think of ourselves as continual learners in an ever changing, inter-related ecology of learning in which even our own changing understanding affects and is conditioned by the changing position of understanding of the others with whom we interact, even marginally.

CONCLUSION

The concept of a network of different devices that are mutually compatible is combined with mobile access (and therefore situation-based connectivity) to give always-on opportunities for learning. The format of this learning is likely to be a blend of different communications systems, contacts with other knowledgeable people, and multi-disciplinary in its subject contents. Faced with so many possible combinations of learning opportunities everybody in the education process needs to think more carefully about how learning opportunities are structured and managed. We highlight the need for greater recognition at the design stage for learning materials to take advantage of the Internet strengths of interactivity and multiple platforms for information flow and storage. Learning providers need to build on the multiplicity and connectivity of platforms that users already employ (e.g., CD ROM, + ebook + audio support) and improving the comfort factor of new technologies for learning so that the learning experience is less dependent on the place (classroom or work) or even the means (or devices) of communication with peers and tutors. There needs to be more recognition given to the reality that personal communications are increasingly able to be mobile and operate through an infrastructure of networks that can pervade every aspect of our lives. This will encourage a blurring between formal and informal learning activities, and raise the value of the latter when such opportunities are linked and clustered in mutually supportive ways. We call this a learning ecology. These changes also bring potential disbenefits but we suggest that in an age of pervasive connectivity the new technological literacy will also require a new etiquette for learning that understands that "always-on" does not necessarily mean "always-answered."

CHAPTER 8

Informal Learning

INTRODUCTION

In this chapter we step outside the highly structured system of formal education to explore ways that people learn through informal and non-formal learning networks. Estimates vary about how much we learn informally compared with learning through recognized courses. One study claims we learn 80% of what we know by informal means (Cross, 2003), whereas another claims that all learning takes place within social organizations or communities which are formalized structures (Billett, 2001). What is not in doubt is that we learn more, and more memorably, in informal settings (McGivney, 1999; Mocker & Spear, 1982). The contention of this chapter is that opportunities for informal learning have been significantly increased in the Connecticon and we need to understand this in order to see how to

"ACTUALLY THIS IS A VERY EXPERIMENTAL COLLEGE. WE HAVE NO CURRICULUM AND NO CLASSES. HOW IT WORKS, ESSENTIALLY, IS IF YOU WANT TO LEARN SOMETHING, YOU GO SOMEPLACE AND YOU LEARN IT."

Source: London Mathematical Society Newsletter. © Sidney Harris

adapt formal learning to work in harmony with informal and non-formal learning.

The phrase, the death of the course, began appearing several years ago and was used as a wake-up call to conventional educational providers.

> Knowledge can be packaged in many ways. The historically most common knowledge package "the course" is dying. We have the Internet to blame, or thank, depending on your orientation.[1]

Learning from websites and online discussion groups is very different from the orientation of formal courses, where stress is laid on learning everything step by step, just in case one needs it later or for the exam. By contrast informal learning is just-in-time and just the amount necessary to put to immediate use. We will look at definitions of formal versus informal learning in the next section, but it is clear that previous themes of the book are beginning to inter-relate. Pervasive learning can provide connectivity to formal courses, but its most exciting applications are in a whole range of informal settings. Learning objects, bite-sized chunks of learning material, can also be part of a formal course, but there are many instances of informal, learning objects that give rise to "accidental" learning. Informal learning from online interaction is also a force for major change in the "source" of a great deal of learning. Open courseware, a concept in which educational providers make their teaching material freely available online (though without tutoring or other support), provides another opportunity for self-directed learning.

INFORMAL LEARNING AND NON-FORMAL LEARNING

A classic definition of informal learning is the following:

> Informal learning, in contrast with formal learning, occurs outside formal classroom settings and is not part of a school program, activity, or assignment. Informal learning is voluntary, self-directed, lifelong, and motivated mainly by intrinsic interests, curiosity, exploration, fantasy, task completion, and social interaction. Informal learning can be linear or non-linear and often is self-paced and visual- or object-oriented. It provides an experiential base and motivation for further activity and learning. The outcomes of an informal learning experience in, for example, science, mathematics, and technology (SMT) include a better understanding of concepts, topics, processes, and thinking in scientific and technical disciplines, as well as increased knowledge about career opportunities in those fields.[2]

Other writers claim that the distinctions between these categories are not nearly so clear-cut and that most definitions (and the one just given is typical of this) carry value assumptions, implicit or explicit, that one form, either formal or informal learning, is inherently superior—sometimes morally, sometimes in terms of effectiveness (Colley, Hodkinson, & Malcolm, 2002).

Some analysts use the terms informal and non-formal learning interchangeably and usually define them by contrast to formal learning. Non-formal learning is a short-hand term for the kind of learning that takes place when people visit museums, zoos and cultural events etc. Informal learning grows out of spontaneous situations such as conversations, physical activities and social interactions. By contrast, formal learning has the following attributes:

- A prescribed learning framework.
- An organized learning event or package.
- The presence of a designated teacher or trainer.
- The award of a qualification or credit.
- The external specification of outcomes (Eraut, 2000).

European policy makes a distinction between non-formal and informal learning based on the intention of the learner: informal learning results from activities in daily life at work, at home, at leisure; non-formal learning is intentional on the part of the learner and structured in terms of learning objectives, but is not provided by a recognized education or training institution (European Commission, 2001).

In reality, most analysts admit that the boundaries between formal, non-formal and informal learning are blurred and can only be meaningfully drawn in relation to particular contexts. It is more useful to talk about dimensions of formality and to look at ways in which these aspects inter-relate.

LEARNING THROUGH ONLINE COMMUNITIES

One of the most obvious ways in which the Connecticon is providing a whole new range of learning opportunities is through group interactions on the web. While online community is being exploited by formal education as we saw in Chapters Two and Three, informal learning through online communities is a much larger phenomenon.

Online communities have been categorized according to the following four types:

- **Geographic**—defined by a physical location like a city or region.

- **Demographic**—defined by age, gender, race or nationality.
- **Topical**—defined by shared interest, like a fan club, hobby group or professional organization.
- **Activity-Based**—defined by a shared activity like shopping, investing, playing games or making music (Kim, 2000, p. 5).

An example of a "topical" community with strong learning elements was the website Ancientsites, created by Cybersites and was an online community of people interested in Ancient History. It allowed a user to join, becoming a member of a particular family of a city. There were many families within the cites of Rome, Athens, Egypt, Tara, Machu Picchu, Babylon, and New York (for those not as interested in Ancient history, but American).

Once a member, you could join other groups, again organized into cities, or take part in discussions on their family boards or on the global boards. There were also chat rooms, quizzes and games available. You were given a homesite, which was made up of an entrance, a courtyard, a library and a study, which could be changed however you wanted, and you could leave other people messages at their homes, or telegram them if they were online as well. Ancientsites was closed on March 30, 2001, as Cybersites was no longer financially able to maintain the site.

An example of a demographic community is iVillage, which started as a focused support site for new parents but grew to become The Women's Network, a demographically targeted community with channels designed to appeal to the different issues, interest, and concerns that women have. Here is an extract from the iVillage UK welcome page:

> Welcome to our thriving network for women. From down-to-earth advice to friendly support, iVillage is here to make your life easier. Whether you need to get **in shape**, get a **new job**, get a **boyfriend**, get a **car**, get **out of debt**, get **healthy**, get **pretty**, get **pregnant** or get **dinner-on-the-go**, we're here to help.
>
> Whatever you're going through, be it your first boyfriend or your first baby you are not alone. If you want to talk to real women, check out our **community message boards**. We have over 100, covering a whole spectrum of life issues. If you want a laugh, a cry, some advice or just a good old gossip, then make the **iVillage community** your first port of call.[3]

Finally, an example of an activity-based community is GeoCities. The site was founded in 1995 to address the need of users who wanted to create their own web pages but lacked the technical skills to do it themselves. GeoCities soon became one of the largest and fastest-growing communities on the web. It continues to focus on making page building easy and accessible to everyone.

Yahoo! GeoCities Free

Publish your resumé, share family photos, or connect with others who share your interests. Choose the point-and-click PageBuilder or step-by-step PageWizards for easy web pages. Upload files from your computer or customize your own HTML with File Manager. See what the Web is all about.[4]

These examples show that online communities are far from static; they are in a continuous process of evolution.

Arguably the most significant area of online community resulting in informal learning outcomes is the health sector.

In the mid and late 1990s, the general public started to realize that via the Internet they could get information about health issues. Dramatic headlines touting this capability began to appear in *USA Today*, the *New York Times*, the British newspaper *The Times* and other national and local newspapers. On Wednesday, July 14, 1999, for example, *USA Today* published a special report entitled "The Internet Changes Medicine" that contained articles with titles such as: "Net Empowering Patients," "Millions Scour the Web for Find Medical Information," and "A Network of Support." USA Today claimed that "In ever growing numbers, patients clutching Internet printouts and a list of smart questions are marching into doctors' offices nationwide" (Davis & Miller, 1999). It is anticipated in the year 2000, that more than 33 million Americans will have researched a medical problem on the Web "The Internet is going to irrevocably affect how patients and doctors interact. This is not going to go away." (Davis & Miller, quoted in Preece, 2000, p. 37)

Preece goes on to point out that patients who go online for health-related information want several things: to understand their problems better; to find information about diseases and treatments; to get support from others; to help fellow sufferers; to feel less afraid and so on. Web sites offer some information, but online communities are more personal resources. Patients can interact with each other and in some cases with professionals (Preece, 2000, p. 38).

INFORMAL LEARNING IN THE WORKPLACE

Many of the uses of the Connecticon are simply replications online of activities that were previously carried out face-to-face. Examples of this in the workplace are:

- Online mentoring (which has the advantage that mentor and mentee need not be co-located.

- Online computer-based training (which is much cheaper than stand-up training and allows learners to study in their own time, but employee acceptance and effectiveness are questionable).
- Email (which replaces paper memos).

However, a sign of the maturation of the Connecticon is the fact that there are a growing number of "unique to the Connecticon" activities that are beginning to appear. One of these is blogging, or web-logging.

What began as a niche activity amongst computer geeks, has been taken up by the business world as the latest informal knowledge management tool. In some cases it is used to share information, discuss clients and projects, and record individual employee ideas and reflections. Some bloggers list their sites on their business cards and other marketing material, but like all blogs, business blogs are promoted mostly through links on other blogs. People who read one blog are likely to read others, so bloggers often endorse sites about related topics. Some business blogs provide a way for companies to update consumers on movements within their firm and products being developed. Research companies such as Gartner Inc. and Jupitermedia Corp. have analysts who keep blogs on issues affecting the industries they study.

Some of the most effective company blogs are posted on internal networks, or intranets. These can help different business divisions connect or allow employees from disparate offices to share information when working together on a big project. Top corporate executives can use blogs as a way to develop relationships with employees, even if it is a mostly one-way conversation.

Another type of informal online learning is the distributed discussion group. These have not always been successful:

> Many intranet-based online communities have failed miserably. To begin with, some managers treated such communities and discussion groups in a cynical manner. They looked at them and saw a cheap way to spread knowledge throughout the organization. All you had to do was install some discussion software. The knowledge sharing would just flow and flow. Of course, it didn't happen that way. There was an early burst of enthusiasm and then people got on with their real jobs. (McGovern, 2003)

However, there are also very notable successes. One of these is Shell which has a range of expert discussion groups, properly moderated and based on knowledge sharing. What makes Shell's online discussions work, where others fail, is the endorsement given throughout the organization to the power of online groups, the value of story-telling as a vehicle for knowledge sharing, and the efficacy of informal learning (see case study box below).

The power of self-organizing groups working together in the Connecticon, is beginning to be recognized by others as well:

[There is] an emerging understanding of how people interact in informal groups to solve complex problems may profoundly influence how we organize and manage corporations, how we hire and train people and what technology we equip them with. Johnson argues that self-organizing groups of "average" people can solve complex problems better than experts can. Challenges today—such as managing a global economy, fighting terrorism or optimizing supply chain operations—are more complex and more distributed than problems were 20 years ago, and so they are less amenable to top-down solutions by "experts."

"The big 'Aha!' for the Internet is that it has become all about a social process," Johnson says. "Every major technological success in the public in the last 50 years—cars, phones, beepers, cell phones, Internet—has been about social connection. They all enhance our ability to connect in some way and are successful because they contribute to the symbiotic intelligence process. But because we do not view society as a self-organizing entity, we only see the advantages to the individual, not the whole."

Johnson says the U.S. shot forward economically during the 1990s while Japan stagnated because the U.S. has a much higher implementation of IT. The worker productivity increases that have driven the U.S. economy can't be easily explained by academics and economists because traditional models see the world as a top-down-driven place operating on known rules. The Internet provides a hidden but vital mechanism that the models overlook, Johnson says. Managers can stimulate the creation of symbiotic intelligence by becoming enablers more than decision-makers, he adds. They can do so by encouraging the use of the Internet, especially e-mail; by flattening the organization while relying less on formal training and expert advice; and by encouraging expression and risk-taking. Managers also should define groups of people with highly diverse personalities and experiences, because diversity accelerates the creation of symbiotic intelligence, he says. (Anthes, 2001)

The lesson for IT managers is to invite diversity and to promote opportunities for informal interaction.

Stories from the Edge:
Story-Telling and its Role in Managing Shell's Knowledge

Story-telling is gaining increasing acceptance as a means of communicating about business. The tradition of an oral narrative history that records and hands down learning, insight or collective revelations still thrives in social communities and Shell has found it particularly effective in helping change our business mindset and improve our knowledge practice.

The power of a good story well told can inspire innovation, personal challenge and professional breakthrough. Stories can encourage us to change, to think "out of our boxes," to seek the aid of others in leveraging our own efforts. For these reasons we have embraced story-telling within Shell Exploration and Production as a means of helping shape our knowledge-sharing culture.

Through computer-enabled global knowledge networks among its professional disciplines, Shell EP has made knowledge flow more easily around its global enterprise.

One aspect of the growth of virtual communities, both internally to companies and as part of the growth of e-business, is the re-emergence of many of the characteristics of the oral cultures that preceded the birth of scientific rationalism, itself enabled by the invention of a printing press. Electronic communication is more conversational, more immediate and more direct. In this context it is not surprising that the story telling skills of previous oral traditions are coming into their own in the new age of uncertainty that we are now entering. The capability of an organization to create its own stories and through that creation to define its culture and place within its chosen environment is key.

Stories from the Edge: Managing Knowledge through New Ways of Working within Shell's Exploration and Production Business, November 2001

LIFE-LONG LEARNING

The notions of lifelong and just-in-time learning have been in the literature for at least 10 years—since the development of online computer-based training and information sources on the Internet. At the root of both concepts is the growing responsibility of the employee to maintain employability, and to do this in ever decreasing amounts of time.

The term just-in-time learning, derives from the manufacturing and production sector, where it has been successful in driving down costs and increasing efficiencies. However, as applied to learning, the momentum behind this banner has increased and perhaps been overtaken with predictions of the "death of the course." Many academic and training courses have been condemned as just-in-case-learning, whereas what is needed is just-for-me learning.

What is the essence of a just-in-time or lifelong learner? John Seeley Brown says it is information navigation:

> The real literacy of tomorrow entails the ability to be your own personal reference librarian—to know how to navigate through confusing, complex information spaces and feel comfortable doing so. "Navigation" may well be the main form of literacy for the 21st century. (Brown, 2000, p. 14)

Brown goes on to endorse discovery-based learning and learning which is situated in action.

> It becomes as much social as cognitive; it is concrete rather than abstract, and it becomes intertwined with judgment and exploration. As such, the Web becomes not only an informational and social resource but a learning medium where understandings are socially constructed and shared. In that medium, learning becomes a part of action and knowledge creation. (Brown, 2000, p. 14)

In IT skills education, this is already happening. If you want to learn the latest techniques in, say, .net technology, there is no alternative but to learn it collaboratively on the Internet, and hundreds of programmers are doing so. Potential employers of this highly paid skill have to find their own ways to measure the outcome of such self-regulated learning.

In fact, all the major computer manufacturers have responded to the needs of the just in time learner. For example, in 1998, Microsoft Corporation launched Microsoft® Seminar Online, which provides IT professionals and developers with instant access to technical education via the World Wide Web. The free service delivered a virtual seminar experience on the Web with presentations given by Microsoft product development teams and field systems engineers. Seminar Online was designed to help users gain a better understanding of a wide range of Microsoft technologies, solutions and programs and to maximize their investments in information technology by teaching ways to use products to their fullest capacity. The user is in control of the learning experience with the ability to watch a full-length presentation or to select specific content.

There is general agreement about the growing need for lifelong learning particularly in relation to the workplace. Increasing competitiveness, efficiency and a growing global context are some of the reasons given for the new emphasis on learning. The evidence about the extent to which this notion is endorsed in the workplace is, however, mixed. There are examples of workplaces which value and promote workplace learning as well as those where learning is not treated seriously.

In this light it is no surprise to observe the convergence of work and learning, and the adoption of new forms of lifelong learning, both for staff development and for personal pleasure (edutainment and simple leisure activities).

Sugata Mitra has a PhD in physics and heads research efforts at New Delhi's NIIT, a fast-growing software and education company with sales of more than $200 million and a market cap over $2 billion. But Mitra's passion is computer-based education, specifically for India's poor. He believes that children, even terribly poor kids with little education, can quickly teach themselves the rudiments of computer literacy. The key, he contends, is for teachers and other adults to give them free rein, so their natural curiosity takes over and they teach themselves. He calls the concept "minimally invasive education."

To test his ideas, Mitra 13 months ago launched something he calls "the hole in the wall experiment." He took a PC connected to a high-speed data connection and imbedded it in a concrete wall next to NIIT's headquarters in the south end of New Delhi. The wall separates the company's grounds from a garbage-strewn empty lot used by the poor as a public bathroom. Mitra simply left the computer on, connected to the Internet, and allowed any passerby to play with it. He monitored activity on the PC using a remote computer and a video camera mounted in a nearby tree.

What he discovered was that the most avid users of the machine were ghetto kids aged 6 to 12, most of whom have only the most rudimentary education and little knowledge of English. Yet within days, the kids had taught themselves to draw on the computer and to browse the Net. Some of the other things they learned, Mitra says, astonished him.

The physicist has since installed a computer in a rural neighborhood with similar results. He's convinced that 500 million children could achieve basic computer literacy over the next five years, if the Indian government put 100,000 Net-connected PCs in schools and trained teachers in some basic "noninvasive" teaching techniques for guiding children in using them. Total investment required, he figures: Around $2 billion.

Figure 8.1   The author's photograph of the site of the first Indian Hole in the Wall.

What gave Mitra the idea of giving slum kids access to the Internet? It was a social observation rather than a scientific one, says Mitra. Any parent who had given his child a computer would invariably remark to me about it. I could hardly ever find an exception. Within a very short period of time, the parent would be claiming that the child was a genius with a computer. When I poked a little further, I invariably found that the child was doing things with the computer that the parent didn't understand.

I asked myself whether the child was really doing something exceptional or if what we were seeing was adult incomprehension. If the adult was simply underestimating the child's ability to cope with a computer, then that should happen with any child. And I asked myself, "Why then would we want to use the same teaching methods for children as we use for teaching adults?"

At first, I tested my ideas with children who were easily available—children at the company here, whose parents are in our executive group.

Then we tried this "hole in the wall" concept, where we put a high-powered Pentium computer with a fast Internet connection into a wall and let [slum] children have access to it with no explanation whatsoever. To be very brief on what happened, the results have been uniform every time we've done this experiment. You get base level computer literacy almost instantly. By computer literacy, I mean what we adults define as computer literacy: The ability to use the mouse, to point, to drag, to drop, to copy, and to browse the Internet.

The children create their own metaphors to do this. To give you an idea of what I mean, a journalist came up to one of these kids and asked him, "How do you know so much about computers?" The answer seemed very strange to her because the kid said, "What's a computer?" The terminology is not as important as the metaphor. If they've got the idea of how a mouse works and that the Internet is [like a wall they can paint on], who cares if they know that a computer is called a computer and a mouse is called a mouse? In most of our classes here at NIIT, we spend time teaching people the terminology and such. That seems irrelevant to me with these children.

But we also found that they would tend to plateau out. They would surf the Web—Disney.com is very popular with them because they like games. And they would use [Microsoft] Paint. It's very, very popular with all of them.

Because these are deprived children who do not have easy access to paper and paint. Every child likes to paint, so they would do it with that program. However, that's all they could do. So I intervened, and I played an MP3 [digital-music file] for them. They were astonished to hear music come out of the computer for the first time. They said, "Oh, does it work like a TV or radio?" I said, in keeping with my approach, "Well, I know how to get there but I don" know how it works." Then I [left].

As I would have expected, seven days later they could have taught me a few things about MP3. They had discovered what MP3 was, downloaded free players, and were playing their favorite songs. As usual, they didn't know what any of it was called. But they would say, "if you take this little box, and you drag this file into this box, it plays music." They had found out where all the Hindi music was on the Web and had pulled it out.

I don't wish to claim that this shows anything more or less than what it has shown, which is that curious kids in groups can train themselves to operate a computer at a basic level. In doing so, they also can get a generally good idea about the nature of browsing and the nature of the Internet . . . And, therefore, if they view these things as worth learning, no formal infrastructure is needed [to teach them].

Now, that's a big deal, because everyone agrees that today's children must be computer-literate. If computer literacy is defined as turning a computer on and off and doing the basic functions, then this method allows that kind of computer literacy to be achieved with no formal instruction. Therefore any formal instruction for that kind of education is a waste of time and money. You can use that time and money to have a teacher teach something else that children cannot learn on their own. If I could make them curious enough, then all the content they need is out there. The greatest expert on earth on viscosity probably has his papers up there on the Web somewhere. Creating content is not what's important. What is important is infrastructure and access . . . The teacher's job is very simple. It's to help the children ask the right questions.

At first, I made a Hindi interface for the kids, which gave them links for hooking up with Web sites in their own language. I thought it would be a great hit. Guess what they did with it? They shut it down and went back to Internet Explorer. I realized that they may not understand the dictionary meaning of [English] words, but they have an operational understanding. They know what that word does. They don't know how to pronounce F-I-L-E, but they know that within it are options of saving and opening up files. . . .

The fact that the Internet is in English will not stop them from accessing it.

They invent their own terminology for what's going on. For example, they call the pointer of the mouse sui, which is Hindi for needle. More interesting is the hourglass that appears when something is happening. Most Indians have never heard of an hourglass. I asked them, "What does that mean?" They said, "It's a damru," which is Hindi for Shiva's drum. [The God] Shiva holds an hourglass—shaped drum in his hand that you can shake from side to side. So they said the sui became a damru when the "thing" [the computer] was doing something.[5]

EDUTAINMENT

The term edutainment (and sometimes infotainment) refers to a growing range of informal education opportunities provided in the Connecticon which combine in differing amounts, learning with fun. Good examples are the public broadcasting authorities such as PBS in the States and the BBC in the UK. They supplement their broadcasts with informative websites where people can interact with program producers, stars or teachers and access background information and follow-up activities.

Examples from the BBC include:

Collaborative Online Story.   This activity involves using a simple website to create a story to which several people can contribute. It develops writing and creative writing skills, understanding of simple web publishing and online co-operation.

Creating a Simple Website.   Lots of information about creating a website with your learners.

Logon to Launch.   This outlines how seven UK online centers went online together on 13th February 2002 to participate in the launch of the High Trees UK online Center. The procedure can form a model of synchronous (real time) links between centers for other special events.

Money Matters to Me.   Money matters to me is an exciting way to understand the different aspects of personal and practical, "day to day" finance. This resource will help you to understand financial matters that are relevant to you and to take control of your money on a day to day basis.[6]

Another example of edutainment is the plethora of semi-educational games which are available. The application of connected electronic games environments to "real life" educational events, including general election results, in-depth news coverage, online simulations, and military or medical training illustrate just some of the informal opportunities for learning not previous available.

Games represent an informal learning environment. It is not unusual for young people to spend 50, 60, 70 hours or more in a particular virtual world playing a game. It might also take 60 hours or so to read "War and Peace." One difference is that games provide a "multi-sensorial" environment. The students are there in body as well as in spirit, and hence memory is enhanced. An increasing number of researchers and educators are considering gaming as a means of teaching this next generation of students. (Oblinger, 2004)

Steve Jones notes:

- Sixty-five percent of those surveyed are regular or occasional game players.
- Games are part of their multi-tasking environment; students will play games while visiting with friends, listening to music or doing assignments. In observations, male students were frequently seen to have online games open alongside their assignments.
- Students integrate games into their lives, playing between classes or while socializing. Students were observed to stop by computer labs for after-class or pre-dinner gaming sessions. Games are seen as a way to spend time with friends (Jones, 2003).

Games have many attributes that are associated with how people learn.

- **Activates prior learning**:   Games require facts. In some cases games are based on understanding topics such as mythology, geology, meteorology, science or history. Players must use previously learned information and learn new facts to move to higher levels of gameplay.
- **Context**:   Context is important in games. Knowing what information or techniques to apply in which situations enables greater success.
- **Feedback and assessment**:   Games provide ample feedback on the player's progress. Scoring, reaching different levels and ultimately winning provide rich feedback and assessment. (Online help can provide just-in-time remediation, as well.)
- **Transfer**:   Games require transfer of learning from other venues— life, school and other games. Being able to see the connection and transfer existing learning to a unique situation is part of gameplay.
- **Experiential**:   Games are inherently experiential. Those who play games engage multiple senses. For each action, there is a reaction. Feedback is swift. Learning is often by trial and error: hypotheses are tested and users learn from the results.
- **Social**:   Games are often social environments, sometimes involving large distributed communities (Oblinger, 2004).

Online, informal opportunities to learn while playing are a phenomenon that we cannot ignore. Games are changing the nature of learning and affecting attention spans; they demand multi-tasking, and experiential and collaborative activity.

Behind the Broadcast: Multimedia and Multicultural

The ubiquity of online access has been relatively slow to integrate with mass communications broadcasting on television and radio, but we are on the cusp of a major social breakthrough. The connections between a broadcast event and the online world were initially limited to the occasional program offering to extend its use of telephone and fax to include an email address that viewers/listeners could use to communicate with the program makers. Mobile phone text messages are now also being encouraged. More recently web sites for some radio channels have enabled global live audiences (through Internet radio) and also the re-play of programs on demand by clicking selections from the playlist. Interactive television has ushered in a new era of viewing that enables the viewer to watch different programs simultaneously on multiple windows, as well as giving 24/7 access, replay on demand, and specialist commentary on key events such as news, politics, sports. Broadcasting companies like the BBC have invested hugely in both digital program distribution and the development of their online content. The next phase, so far largely only in the planning stage, is for other companies to provide online materials that complement and/or add value to the broadcast programs. This will not only significantly extend the shelf-life of broadcast programs (shown once, perhaps repeated, and then forgotten) but will also allow specialist, minority, and alternative interpretation of mainstream broadcasts. It will allow, for example, a more in-depth commentary of a current affairs television program to be presented in a minority language; it will allow contrasting commentaries to be presented side by side to significantly enhance the depth of perspective; and it will allow many layers of considerable detail to be added for specialists that would be inappropriate and impossible to provide on a short peak-time popular entertainment channel. Not only will this present considerable challenges for the broadcasting corporation (who by-and-large have an editorial monopoly on what they show and how they choose to present it) but may also have a democratizing influence on the generation of popular media. We may see the growth of media-libraries, that cut and re-use valuable materials recorded and broadcast one, in the same way as we have seen the growth of educational reusable learning objects. Local news and minority interest activities may be able to capture small but significant markets, piggy-backing on the mass dissemination of popular media programs, with and/or without the approval of the broadcasting corporation. The potential for educational use is vast.

Educational Institutions and Informal Learning

There are a few signs that formal educational institutions are beginning to respond to the evident success of informal online learning. The most obvious is probably the interest that academics are taking in emulating computer games as a way of generating the same enthusiasm amongst learners in academic subjects. There is also interest in the skills that young people are developing from their recreational uses of networking:

- Common interest communities (hobby sites, e-groups discussing movies).
- Competition and game sites (networked multi-player games, entering competitions).
- File download sites (Napster, clipart).
- Corporate and ecommerce sites (internet banking, online shopping).
- Information access sites (maps, timetables, White Pages)

Participating in these online networks can allow students to develop many useful skills including database searching, information filtering, data storage and retrieval, critical analysis of resources and effective online communication.... Clearly, such skills are useful for tertiary students from a wide range of backgrounds from general study habits required by undergraduate students to the more refined research expertise required for postgraduate study (Northcote & Kendle, 2001, p. 1).

Some universities directly address the issue of informal learning on their public websites. For example, MIT:

Playful Inventions and Exploration network, MIT The PIE Network brings together the hands-on inquiry approach of science museums with the learning philosophy from the MIT Media Lab known as "Constructionism."[7]

and the University of Wisconsin:

Our challenge is to make the University of Wisconsin-Madison a more welcoming place for the informal learner. The UW-Madison's research mission can be viewed as a process of informal learning: the researcher independently investigates a question of interest. Ultimately, we envision UW-Madison as a model for an intentional process of leveraging the formal resources of a major educational and scientific research institution into a thriving resource for informal science education for learners of all ages.[8]

Nevertheless, most universities and most instructors need to wake up to the realities of how most learning is now taking place. They need to see the Connecticon as an ally not an enemy that is eroding traditional ways of knowing.

Adults learn by doing. Knowles' andragogical model established this. Research has confirmed this practical preference. Universities use formal courses to teach 16 million Americans every year. But more than four times this number—90 million adult Americans—learn without the aid of formal courses each year.

In 1997 The Education Development Center of Massachusetts quantified the amount of career knowledge that the average adult learns not in formal courses or degree programs but from co-workers: a shocking 70%. The Academy of Life enjoys a body of alumni much larger than the Ivy League.

Adults crave education they can grab onto and put to immediate use. They take a pluck-n-play approach to knowledge. They pluck what they need to know from books, online discussion lists, Web sites, and the brains of their co-workers. This contrasts to the historical orientation of the formal course, where stress is laid on learning everything from A-to-Z, step-by-step, just-in-case one might need it later. E-learning programs can and should cultivate the native each-one-teach one principle that is the adult's preferred and richest knowledge conduit. Formal courses are optional under this approach. The Internet has changed the way knowledge is packaged.[9]

As content—knowing that—becomes less useful than process—knowing how, formal education needs to foster a different kind of learning: a network of facilitators, peers, resources and activities which help learners develop the skills, the cognitive approaches and understanding to master their chosen field.

The Dangers of Informal Learning

More information is not always synonymous with more understanding. Increasing access to information through the ubiquity of the internet has been paralleled by a growing mistrust in traditional institutions and figures of authority. A World Economic Forum survey reports that over half the respondents have little or no trust in national parliaments or in government leaders (Alakeson et al., 2004). The reasons behind this are intricate and involved, associated with grand processes of social transformation and economic restructuring, but the Connecticon has certainly played a major role in this mistrust. One example of this is the increasingly common situation in which patients confront their doctors with sheets of information on their condition which they have downloaded from websites or health support groups. They challenge the doctor's opinion based on their online research. Of course it is a positive development when people take an active interest in their own health, but as is well known, a little information can be a dangerous thing! An increasing number of online communities now support question-and-answer sessions with real doctors, but some doctors do not like this practice either, arguing that online doctors do not see their patients or know their backgrounds. Patients need to learn to become discerning consumers of medical information (Preece, 2000, p. 39).

Online groups can provide many benefits for participants who are increasingly turning to virtual communities to provide a way of generating trust and wider social value just as local geographical communities have always done in the past. However, both kinds of communities can suffer from a silo mentality that increases prejudice, narrow-mindedness, exclusivity and ignorance. Exposure to a diversity of opinion, people and information sources, is the antidote. This antidote is certainly available in the Connecticon, but the bewildering variety of different communities of interest online can lead people to "retreat" to small corners of this vast information network. One report concludes that:

> Electronic networks are most powerful when embedded into existing social networks, where the trust needed for information to flow already exists and can be built on. As ICT becomes an everyday part of people's lives, there's a clear trend towards a closer connection between virtual community and real world community. ICT is being used to build trust by augmenting real world interaction, unleashing the potential of information on the network to empower individual choices and action. (Alakeson et al., 2003, p. 65)

One of the most beneficial aspects of informal learning is that it is flexible and responsive to new and changing circumstances. As it occurs over a period of time, it is capable of being deep rooted and adaptable to an individual's needs and situation. However, there are negative effects as well, and in relation to the workplace, it may be too narrowly based. This results in the employee learning the skills of doing a particular task or part of a task which may not then be transferable. It may not lead to a consciously possessed ability or skill, and it may encourage the employee to learn bad habits or the wrong lessons without being aware of the fact. These negative effects can be counteracted by a learning culture in the organization, for example, through the provision of time to enable reflection and discussion, through an acceptance of mistakes as an inevitable part of learning, and of course through an open and honest attitude to communication.

Finally, there is the issue of time-wasting and miss-use of company resources. A recent survey by Websense found that staff were spending an average of 3.4 hours of their working week using the Web for non-work reasons. One commentator notes that the online community idea can get seriously out-of-hand in organizations and might as well carry a sign saying "wasting time at work." He asks:

> Is it the job of your organization to help staff sell their second-hand cars? Should you have access to weather and horoscopes? Should you help staff book holidays or order groceries? (McGovern, 2003)

CONCLUSION

Are we predicting the end of formal education? No, certainly not, but formal education needs shaking up, in order to understand the impact of the

Connecticon on learning and on the habits, interests and existing skills of learners.

Are we claiming that the Connecticon actually creates new learning? At the technology level, of course not. What it does is allow collective meaning to emerge.

> Communities are neither designed nor do they just emerge. How software is designed affects community development just as the architecture of a house affects those who live in it. How people interact in a community shapes its long-term evolution. And though people's behaviour cannot be controlled, it can be influenced. (Preece, 2000, p. 6)

The Connecticon represents an unprecedented resource for learning, in terms of the amount of information that is readily available. However, it is the interaction around information that is much more significant. People are empowered by the Connecticon in ways they have never been before. John Seeley Brown predicts:

> My belief is that not only will the Web be as fundamental to society as electrification, but that it will be subject to many of the same diffusion and absorption dynamics as that earlier medium. We're just at the bottom of the S-curve of this innovation, a curve that will have about the same shape as with electrification, but a much steeper slope than before. As this S-curve takes off, it creates huge opportunities for entrepreneurs. It will be entrepreneurs, corporate or academic, who will drive this chaotic, transformative phenomenon, who will see things differently, challenge background assumptions, and bring new possibilities into being. Our challenge and opportunity, then, is to foster an entrepreneurial spirit toward creating new learning environments—a spirit that will use the unique capabilities of the Web to leverage the natural ways that humans learn. (Brown, 2000, p. 13)

NOTES

1. http://www.geteducated.com/vug/nov01/vug1101.htm
2. http://www.deltasee.org/trainers/pdfs/Chapter%204%20Overview%20of%20Informal%20Science%20Education.pdf
3. http://www.ivillage.co.uk/ivillageuk/editor/articles/0,10231,177714_186871.html
4. http://geocities.yahoo.com/ps/learn2/HowItWorks4_Free.html
5. From a Businessweek Online Daily Briefing, March 2, 2000. Edited by Paul Judge.
6. http://www.helpisathand.gov.uk/learning/learning/informal/
7. http://www.media.mit.edu/research/2003-10web.pdf
8. http://www.biotech.wisc.edu/Education/alliance/informal.html
9. http://www.geteducated.com/vug/nov01/vug1101.html

CHAPTER 9

Learning to Learn How to Learn

W hen Richard Dawkins, the British zoologist invented the term "meme" in his 1976 book on genetics, he created a self-replicating idea that defined its very own existence. Initially he coined the term simply to describe a "unit of cultural transmission" that could replicate and "propagate themselves in the meme pool by leaping from brain to brain via a process which, in the broad sense, can be called imitation" (Dawkins, 1978, p. 206). The analogy with genes was deliberate, and

"EINSTEIN!!! Stop fooling around and pay attention!"

Source: Almedia Cartoons at: http://www.almediacartoons.com

though *exact* comparisons in the behavior of genes and memes, their methods of replication and so on, may not be identical, there is enough similarity to provide us with a useful way of exploring the transmission of culture, ideas, and innovations. There has been much written on memes since this time (there is even an academic journal of the science of memetics[1]) and we will draw attention to some of the literature, but it seems relatively little of this has been applied to how we learn in an Internet-connected society, so we will focus on that in this chapter.

The Connecticon: Learning for the Connected Generation, pages 129–142
Copyright © 2004 by Information Age Publishing

Before we start, we should have a clear idea of what we are calling a meme. There are several different refinements of definition but a basic description is a:

> contagious idea that replicates like a virus, passed on from mind to mind. Memes function the same way genes and viruses do, propagating through communication networks and face-to-face contact between people. (Bennahum, 1998)

So the idea of a meme is *itself* a meme—a useful way to describe how some ideas spread and other do not—and this concept is spread (replicated) by repetition, both by those that find the concept useful and also by its detractors.

The definition we prefer is any self-replicating "memetic information in its many forms; including ideas, the brain structures that instantiate those ideas, the behaviors these brain structures produce, and their versions in books, recipes, maps and written music. As long as that information can be copied by a process we may broadly call 'imitation,' then it counts as a meme" (Blackmore, 1999, p. 66). This frees us from the limitations of *how* memes jump from brain to brain, whether by speech, or books, or the Internet to look more closely at what happens when they do so.

This is important to us all because not everything is a meme. Only patterns of information that have the ability to replicate themselves by imitation can be classed as memes, and these have the ability to:

> evolve through adaptive exploration and transformation of an information space through variation, selection, and transmission. . . . Since unlike genes, memes do not come packaged with instructions for their replication, our brains do it for them, strategically, guided by a fitness landscape that reflects both internal drives and a worldview that is continually updated through meme assimilation. (Gabora, 1997)

Like their counterpart, the gene, a meme is either successful or unsuccessful at getting passed on to the next generation. An idea, a piece of music, an image, or a certain style of fashion is neither "good" nor "bad" except in its ability to replicate itself and so survive to produce more replicas, which will in turn have a greater or lesser success in replicating further. In discussing Dawkins ideas of memes as replicators of culture, Blackmore notes three fundamental properties of a good quality replicator:

> fidelity, fecundity, and longevity. This means that a replicator has to be copied accurately, many copies must be made, and the copies must last a long time—although there may be trade-offs between the three. (Blackmore, 1999, p. 58)

Intrinsic in the concept of memes is the notion that they seem to undergo a process that has comparisons with biological evolution, namely the variation, selection, and replication of coded information. Gabora (1997, p. 3) identified four components of a system that are required to enable evolution to occur, these are:

1. A pattern of information.
2. A way to generate variations of the pattern.
3. A rationale for selecting the variations that are adaptive—tend to give better performance than their predecessors in the context of some problem or set of constraints.
4. A way of replicating and transmitting the selected variations.

This is where we can begin to appreciate the role of the Connecticon in the incubation, storage, evolution, and spread of memes. First, the transfer of a meme around the infrastructure of the Connecticon is in a digital format, a very, very high-fidelity format, that as we have seen preserves its integrity not just through time, but also across the range of appliances used to access the Connecticon. This is the so-called "compatibility" issue in information technology, and we are increasingly seeing text, moving images, and sound (music and voice) relayed between different types and generations of devices, such as computers (desk-top, laptop, hand-top) mobile phones, and televisions. We are starting to see the next generation of devices that are embedded in other artefacts of our world, such as wrist-watches, vehicle windscreens, and "smart" paints and fabrics.

Second, the more copies of a meme that are made, the greater probability that the ideas (memes) will spread vertically from one generation to another and horizontally through global society. New memes emerge from the variation of existing ones (cf. genetic mutation) as well as by a recombination of old memes in new ways. From this perspective innovation and entrepreneurial ideas appear to emerge from the overlap (recombination) of two or more memes in a new form that is capable of rapid replication due to the fact that it is particularly well suited for its new situation. In terms of the Connecticon, the first level infrastructure provides an ideal structure to ensure fidelity of the meme, while the human resources of the users at the second level provide the means (and the driving factor) for the introduction of variation. The human interpretation, recombination, mis/understanding, and attempt to apply the information contained in digital memes have the effect of mutation, embellishment, and refinement of the "original" memes. The fast (almost instantaneous) effect of many-to-many digital communications within the Connecticon increases the fecundity of meme transmission, and the hyper-interactivity of level three serves to heighten this further. The meme in the Connecticon is like bacteria introduced into an unhygienic kitchen. It is a fast-breeder for ideas, but as we shall see later the production of ideas is not enough for learning, we need efficient mechanisms to identify, select, and retain memes that are able to help contextualize knowledge into understanding.

From the perspective of the meme, although they rely upon human brains to select, vary, and replicate them, the humans are simply vehicles for the perpetuation of the memes, in exactly the same manner that genes "use" living creatures to perpetuate themselves. The growing science of memetics has attempted to deploy the thinking about memes and how they function to subjects as diverse as the origin of culture and creativity (Gabora, 1997), the efficiency of financial markets (Frank, 1999), and the onslaught (and resistance to) pervasive commercial advertising (Downes, 1999). Some of this thinking has provocative and disturbing conclusions, not the least of which is that rather than humans having created the Internet for our own benefit, it makes more sense "when you think of the memes as having created the Web to aid their own replication, and competing with each other to get your attention" (Blackmore, 1999, p. 217).

MEMES AND LEARNING

So how do all the pieces of this jigsaw puzzle fit together? Memes, individual learning, and the Internet, what are the common links? First of all it is patently obvious that there are more memes available than brains to house them. The successful memes are the ones that are able to replicate, and they do this because of natural selection. The memes that exhibit particular patterns of behavior and/or contain data that is easily replicated (good OR bad) will be the memes that persist to subsequent generations. Understanding therefore becomes a result of competition between memes, and the memes that replicate fastest, with greater fidelity, and greatest longevity will continue to replicate and find their way into our everyday thoughts and fears and patterns of behavior. The very early myths and folk-tales with simple, easily memorable motifs, are able to be applied to very different patterns of behavior in contemporary life and are still able to convey meanings and metaphors despite their obvious lack of logicality.

The difficulty for learning, structured or unstructured, is that the Connecticon is an ideal mechanism for the fast breeding and transfer of ideas, but the speed of propagation and transfer is of a different order of magnitude to the selection and retention of the memes. The users of technology within the Connecticon are the main mechanism for the identification, selection, and replication of memes. The various memes (and their mutations resulting from human mis/interpretation) can be stored and made available in the community memory of the Connecticon, on hard disks and other storage facilities, and made globally available to users of the Connecticon. There is a growing, and almost limitless well of data available, memes of all sorts, good and bad, long-lasting and flash-in-the-pan ideas that will be literally here today and gone tomorrow. So how does the learner make sense of all of this? How does she or he identify and assimilate data and knowledge in a sequential manner that enables the learner to learn, to build understanding, and not simply respond "parrot-fashion" with a "pick-and-mix" bag of ideas that bear no relevance to reality?

To comprehend this, we need to appreciate two other fundamental emergent properties of the Connecticon. The first is the attention economy, and the second is situated learning. We have already made passing mention of the attention economy earlier in this book, but it takes on a new level of meaning in the present context. Quite simply, how do we make sense of all of the millions of memes that bombard us as we move around in the Connecticon? How do we sort out the "useful" ideas from the crazier ideas without rejecting the golden ideas that are eccentric but have the potential to take us off in innovative, unpredictable directions that give rise to new inventions and new ways of thinking? In the attention economy of Goldhaber (1997, 1998a,b) that we touched on briefly in chapter one, we found that information is not in short supply in the Connecticon, but prioritizing this information and giving it the required amount of attention can be a huge difficulty. Viewing the current "information age" from the perspective of the patterns of activity and interrelationships between individuals and groups (enhanced by the hyper-interactivity made possible by the Connection) can give us new insights in how we learn (select, contain, and contextualize information) and how we explain the survival of some memes from generation to generation.

> The parallel I want to draw is that the new kinds of connection that the Net and cyberspace make possible also demand a whole new way of thinking if you are to understand what is going on between people, the kinds of organized effort that are now possible, the motivations that most matter, and a host of other facets of life. (Goldhaber, 1997, p. 3)

It is this ability to command attention that has enabled some aspects of information and ideas to spread around the globe, posing problems for government censors (Watts, 2004) and challenging our staid, conventional thinking on the current constraints of copyright, plagiarism, and intellectual property rights. As it is harder to command attention by simply repeating exactly what has been done before, or trying to tell people information that is already in common circulation, there is an imperative toward originality and innovation. Goldhaber has predicted that due to the ease with which we can use the Connecticon to move information around, contextualize it to our own familiar situations, and through media technology "to look behind the scenes as easily as at them," produces greater accessibility and transparency to knowledge networks.

> This transparency will even more be the case in the very near future, and, as a result, organizations will diminish in importance at rapid pace, relative to the importance of the individuals who are temporarily in them. Even as stable and long-lasting an institution as Harvard will be less its familiar buildings and more the people in the buildings, and the networks of attention among them. And whether these people are physically at Harvard or somewhere else will matter less and less, until the institution loses all coherence, all distinctness from other universities or from any one of hundreds of other organizations which have audiences in common. (Goldhaber, 1997, p. 12)

The implications for this are colossal, and we can see indications of them emerging throughout our society, many of which we have mentioned in this book—e.g., asynchronous and blended learning, education within the work context, course sharing between institutions, the flexibility and re-usability of smaller learning objects, and so on. Lanham noted that:

> In an attention economy, libraries and librarians move center stage. Librarians no longer facilitate thinking done elsewhere. The "thinking" will be the construction of attention-structures, and they—that is to say you—will be in the middle of it. (Lanham, 1994, p. 6)

Further exploring this concept, Lankshear and Knobel note the need to develop further gateways to allow people to give attention to relevant information, "turn it into something useful for users and to enable users to use it more usefully in terms of their wants and goals" (Lankshear & Knobel, 2001, p. 7). A critical issue is the extent to which the university facilitates this role, or provides an impediment by the continued application of outdated learning structures, contextually inappropriate curricula, and elitist notions of the use and function of knowledge.

A consideration of the theory of situated learning can help us to progress from an assimilation of disjointed pieces of information that bombard us with their attention-seeking characteristics, to structured paths of knowledge accumulation that enables us to adjust our world view of ourselves and our environment. Situated learning, as defined by Lave and Wenger (1990) claims that learning normally occurs as a function of the activity, context, and culture in which it occurs. That is, learning is situated in real events and interactive experiences of the individual rather than in abstract knowledge that is out of context for that individual. Social interaction is a critical component of situated learning theory, with learners becoming involved in a "community of practice" that shares similar belief and behaviors with other members of the community. As we have seen in chapter two, communities of practice are themselves complex and interleaved, with all of us having membership of a number of different communities at any one time—e.g., our extended family, our work colleagues, our sports group or fellow musicians, and our local evening class. All and any combination of these might be face-to-face or online. It is not at all uncommon to be speaking on Netmeeting, and to simultaneously have the email "ping" with an incoming message while the phone on the desk rings (or is switched to voicemail) and the mobile phone signals the arrival of a text message.

This "learning by doing" principle is a well-tested tool of adult educators and community development practitioners in their efforts to make learning relevant to people for whom learning is a means to an end (e.g., in "solving" some other problems) rather than an end in itself (Rennie, 1987; Bell et al., 1990; Glen, 1988). In the Connecticon there are simply infinitely more possibilities of exchanging contextually relevant information with other people. We extend our understanding by analyzing what we know about a topic, then sorting through the blizzard of incoming new information (i.e., new to us) to find a piece that "fits" and allows us to attach the new data onto the existing data in our brains to form a new array of data sets that enables us to more fully comprehend the changed context of our situation. Learning in the Connecticon is therefore simply seen to be an enhanced way of building upon experiential learning that community activists have long known. In documenting the work of the Highlander Research and Education Center in Appalachia, Adams commented,

> People learn of unity by acting in unity. They learn of democracy by acting democratically. And each time they do these things as a result of experiences at Highlander they both renew their capacity to act in these ways again and demonstrate the process of education in action. Talk about this process distorts, and is one step removed from the essential element—the people themselves doing. Writing in words about the process is two steps removed. (Adams, 1972)

The Connecticon enables this process to be extended hugely, to include the exchange of intimate, contextual information with people far from our own geographical communities. The academic literature and the Web itself are full of testimonial stories to the importance of peer-to-peer communication for learning—health newsgroups, for instance, frequently emphasize the effects of a cancer patient, or the parent of a child with some life-threatening illness, communicating directly with some unknown person who has experience of a very similar situation. Online communities such as the WELL have established their reputation as electronic portals that provide a gateway to an almost unlimited resource of human experience in the Connecticon that is available for consultation, comparison, and learning.

In our own work we have frequently been surprised when a simple question or request on an electronic mailing list has encouraged the question to be passed from person to person, network to network, resulting in a reply, directly to us, from the person thousands of miles away who first wrote the paper, did the deed, or was at the event in question.

It is critical to appreciate that these learning communities (or Connecticon spaces as we have suggested in chapter two) are ecological systems of complex interaction in their own right. They function within the complex adaptive system of the Connecticon, but at a different level pertinent to their own network functions and level of complexity. Each of these Connecticon spaces (or virtual learning communities if you insist) have their own characteristic emergent properties, many of which will be shared with other Connecticon spaces on their own level, (different to the combination of properties at the whole system level) some properties of which may be unique and provide a signature for *that* group of participants—the quirky combination of properties that makes *this* community *ours*.

A further important point in the theory of situated learning is that it is usually unintentional, rather than deliberate,[2] with learning occurring *because* of our active participation in a process rather than simply the conscious acquisition of random facts and contextually inappropriate information. Anyone who has watched their children learn to play electronic games on the home computer or mobile phone and wondered at their apparently "intuitive" ability to navigate the complex rules of the games will have an inkling of what is happening. The process of meme transfer (learning by imitation) in a context of situated learning (actually doing something that is important to them and their peers) is a powerful stimulant to learning. As we have seen with the hole-in-the-wall situation, and other non-invasive learning experiences, the users (in this case children) do not need to know the technicalities of what they are doing, nor whether the concepts they employ are basic or advanced, merely they that work, and (for them) the cumulative experience is good. A similar case might be made for language learning, in that we effortlessly "absorb" our native tongue from our parents and others in our close community (and this also goes for bilingual communities) whereas we "struggle" to learn a new language in adulthood, yet we are "surprised" when we visit the country and "immerse" ourselves in the culture that our language competence improves with such rapidity.

WEBWORKS OF TRUST

Central to our understanding of how individuals learn in connected societal networks is an appreciation of the importance of trust. In communicating information between individuals of a network, a high degree of worth is often (knowingly and unknowingly) placed upon the information received from sources that have been proven to have been reliable in the past. Growing up within our own families, we begin by placing an implicit trust in our parents, teachers, and elders, only to be disappointed later when some of their information does not match with our own experiences of reality. We then learn to question, challenge, and verify each piece of information that we receive from these sources, the level of our trust (or doubt!) being proportionate to our perceptions of the quality of information that we are fed. The more we search for evidence of this process, the more we find it, leaving some commentators to claim that:

> Trust is more than a highly esteemed value. Along with technology and inno-
> vation, it is one of the most powerful forces driving business today. We are a
> society in search of Trust. The less we find it, the more precious it becomes.
> (Alakeson et al., 2003, p. 59)

Some businesses have sought to maximize the levels of human trust among the network of the members/users as a way to enhance their company status and hence their commercial prospects. The online auction site eBay has attracted millions of users despite the perceived risks and uncertainties in trading goods and money between members of the network that have never met, and may never have any prospects of meeting face-to-face. They have embraced in their business strategy the realization that:

> The most fundamental security issue online is the basic question of trust.
> Users must be able to trust each other in order for meaningful, ongoing
> interaction to occur. (Boyd, 2002, p. 2)

Key to this strategy is the construction of a networked community in such a way that users have self-interested motives to act ethically and honestly in their transactions. Through a system of peer-mediated meritocracy that awards points to buyers and sellers with a higher track record of satisfied deals, together with a transparent approach to business that makes these status levels accessible in full view to other potential dealers, it is possible to make trust estimations on the contributions of complete strangers. We have already mentioned the manner in which Amazon attempts to build trust in their market, first by personalizing your transactions with the company ("Welcome back Frank..." and search tabs with "Frank Rennie's book store"); second by automated product profiling ("customers [like you] who have bought the book that you have just purchased have also bought the following..."); and third by enabling individuals (authors, readers, and purchasers) to submit their own comments or reviews to each item in order to provide a greater level of relatively impartial detail on the value/relevance of the item. Of course there are dangers with this, who is profiling who, are you always aware that each click adds more information on you to a database, and what might all this information be used for? Despite the lack of commercial pressures to adopt the principles of such a system, the universities, and higher education in general, have singularly failed to capitalize on automated ICT systems that would facilitate the enhancement of trust in online learning environments. With specific reference to the facilitation of learning in corporate communities of practice, Gongla and Rizzuto commented that:

> To perform well in this knowledge economy, individuals must constantly apply and add to their own bodies of knowledge. They do this by finding ways to participate on a day-to-day basis in a flow of knowledge that consists, not only of the dissemination of data and printed material, but also of the exchange of ideas with other individuals who have experience and skill related to the same area of work. (Gongla & Rizzuto, 2001, p. 842)

These informal knowledge networks can be crucially important in the management of selective contextual information to facilitate sectoral understanding and situated learning.

In an investigation on information exchange leading to better participation in democratic governance, Jordan et al. (2003) asked how new Internet software and standards could best be deployed to support, self-propagating, self-organized communities that are based on trust. They asked if the Internet could (a) find others with shared affinities, (b) share relevant information and media with one another, and (c) self-organize and more easily form alliances to engage constructively with our neighbors, our fellow, citizens, and our representatives in government? Again it is significant that the mention of educational activities is prominent by its absence. They proposed the creation of an Augmented Social Network (ASN) that would build identity and trust into the architecture of the Internet, predominantly by a combination of automated, as well as human-mediated, exploitation of interactive digital media. The importance of the second level of the Connecticon is explicitly acknowledged with the recognition that;

> In our lives, each of us inhabits a wide range of distinct, independent social networks. As we move between them, we bring with us our unique interests, our experience, knowledge, and relationships. (Jordan et al., 2003, p. 6)

A number of currently available technologies are described by Jordan et al that could help to facilitate online profiling which enables a "persistent identity" to be established for each user. In other words it makes use of a method of recording the users affinities, interests, capabilities, and skills

that would enable other users with similar interests to identify and communicate within like-minded networks. An advantage of such brokering services (automated or human) lies in the power of the network inter-
connectivity to speed up the location and matching of peer-networks,
along with the potential to self-author user profiles to accommodate
changes in user attributes through time, as well as the de-selection of
attributes to reflect privacy wishes. As Nardi and O'Day recognize:

> An information ecology is a system of people, practices, technologies, and
> values in a local environment. Like their biological counterparts, informa-
> tion ecologies are diverse, continually evolving, and complex. (Nardi &
> O'Day, 1999)

The strength of professional networks (formal and informal) for learning has long been recognized as a critical form of social organization, but
some observers have been moved to document their claim that:

> traditional institutional resources are being replaced by resources that work-
> ers mine from their own networks. . . . [leading to] . . . the emergence of per-
> sonal social networks as the main form of social organization in the
> workplace. (Nardi, Whittaker, & Schwartz, 2000, p. 1)

In part these social networks (or *intensional* networks) are promoted by
the breakdown of strong institutional and sectoral ties as corporate structures become bigger, clumsier, less job-demarcated, and less co-located.
Another aspect of the success of these networks, however, is that they are
based around personal selection of co-workers, short/long time contact
projects, and mutual benefits, consistent with the attention economy analysis. These networks require nourishing and frequent updating to be "live"
and efficient, and Nardi and co-workers have suggested that there are
three main tasks that need constant attention:

1. Building a network: Adding new nodes (people) to the network so
   that there are available resources when it comes to conduct joint
   work;
2. Maintaining the network, where a central task is keeping in touch
   with extant nodes;
3. Activating selected nodes at the time the work is to be done (Nardi
   et al., 2000, p. 11).

Finally, with specific reference to this construction of human networks,
it is worth considering the principle of neural networks with a view to
understanding how they find their numerous ways of expression in the

complex adaptive system of the Connecticon. Haykin offers a relatively simple, definition of a neural network viewed as an adaptive machine:

> A neural network is a massively parallel distributed processor made up of simple processing units, which has a natural propensity for storing experiential knowledge and making it available for use. It resembles the brain in two respects:
>
> 1. Knowledge is acquired by the network from its environment through a learning process.
> 2. Interneuron connection strengths, known as synaptic weights, are used to store the acquired knowledge (Haykin, 1999, p. 2).

In particular, the self-organising capacity of the system to select and produce order from randomly incoming pieces of digital information offers significant prospects for a new wave of intelligent data management for peer-to-peer learning. Techniques such as the "self-organising map" present the ability to:

> transform an incoming signal pattern of arbitrary dimension into a one- or two-dimensional discrete map, and to perform this transaction adaptively in a topographically ordered fashion. (Haykin, 1999, p. 446)

This also provides an analysis of the process of formation of the self-organizing map, and three essential emergent properties are noted:

1. **Competition** between the neurons (producing a winning neuron).
2. **Cooperation** between the winning neuron and other neurons in the topological neighborhood.
3. **Synaptic adaptation** of the excited neurons that enables the response of the winning neuron to enhance its response to the subsequent application of a similar input pattern.

It is interesting to speculate on the application of this mechanism within the larger ecology of the Connecticon. Competition is certainly the dominant selective mechanism in the survival and replication of memes and other social learning factors, but so is cooperation (the combination of ideas, and parts of ideas, to make new ideas and concepts better adapted to their new context). Although innovative thinking may be accelerated by competition, at what point does this competition become a limiting factor as compared with the potential benefits of cooperation or collaboration with other successful clusters of competitors? It will be a potentially fascinating region of future research to explore the issues surrounding synaptic adaptation with respect to collaborative learning clusters, innovative research teams, and "think-tank" groups who routinely attempt to reassemble information and learn in novel ways. If synaptic adaptation were to be established to be operatively functional among groups of people as well as groups of neurons we would be on the verge of understanding how mutually supportive networks could help to teach us *how* to learn in any given situation, with concomitant revelations for andragogical processes in lifelong learning. We then truly would be "learning in the networked society."

CONCLUSIONS

The Connecticon provides a new and uniquely efficient vehicle for the transfer, storage, selection, replication, and contextualization of information and knowledge. This is not only because information in the Connecticon is transferred in digital format, but also because these hyper-interactive networks are ideally suited to learning in their most appropriate situations, in the library, office or on the move where people can utilize ideas by "copying the instructions" rather than trying to replicate the product. New ways of looking at the replication, transfer, selection and prioritization of information, such as we have considered from the perspective of memes and in the attention economy, will have a huge impact upon how we design and "deliver" education in the future. Not only does the infrastructure of the Connecticon enable the high-fidelity transfer of digital information, through the human resources of the user interface, this information can mutate, be combined, selected, and replicated for further transfer (including other media outwith Connecticon, such as books, newspapers, and causal conversations.) Implications for reconsidering information ecologies in this manner include the breakdown of organizational barriers to knowledge sharing, and the build-up of personalized networks that are based on social networks of trust. In the search to make sense of the information overload, to identify the good ideas from the bad, and to spot "the next big thing," we should realize that it is not only "good" ideas that can grab our attention, but simply the ideas that are best at replicating themselves. As competing ideas attempt to undermine our trust in others, information from trusted sources becomes even more valuable. Although there are increasingly sophisticated technological tools to identify, transfer, and store relevant ideas, this does not undermine the importance of peer support networks, and only serves to strengthen the role of the tutor/teacher as a facilitator of knowledge sources rather than an oracle. There are suggestions that the effectiveness of these learning networks improves with a balance of competition versus collaboration and with repeated frequent active participation of the members of the network—an interesting new application of the classic philosopher's game theory, "The Prisoner's Dilmma" (Dennett, 2003, p. 147 et seq.).

NOTES

1. See http://jom-emit.cfpm.org
2. Situated learning http://tip.psychology.org/lave.html

CHAPTER 10

Future Pathways for Learning

INTRODUCTION

Throughout the book we have been exploring a variety of ways in which learning—both formal and informal—is evolving due to the technologies and affordances of the Connecticon. The connected age, with its emphasis on knowledge growth and multiple forms of communication, is dependent upon citizens being able to

"It might be some sort of evolution thing. Your baby's navel is an Ethernet port."

Source: Randy Glasbergen at: http://www.glasbergen.com/cat.html

learn effectively. The speed and incessant demand for change are creating a need for formal and informal educational opportunities to become more effective and efficient. Moreover, the social costs of neglecting education exacerbate schisms between those with opportunities for learning and those without. The "have" and "have not" effects are social costs that individuals, as well as society as a whole, can ill afford.

Critics of the overselling of the Web as a force for change have rightly challenged uncritical assumptions about the social and educational implications of the information society and connected generation (Garnham, 2002).

We have tried to present a balanced view of the changes, highlighting both the gains and the losses. However, by focusing solely on the content and processes of learning during the preparation of these chapters, we have continually been surprised ourselves at just how profound and widespread the changes are, not potentially are, but actually are.

It seems very evident from our analysis that these changes, both to the content and the processes of learning, are influenced by three characteristics of the Connecticon:

1. The capacity of the Internet for effective information capture, storage and retrieval.
2. The capacity of the Internet to support, extend and expand communication capabilities of humans in multiple formats across the bounds of time and space.
3. The capability of the Connecticon to create an environment which empowers learners to be more proactive, self-directed and experiential in their learning.

We have made a case for changes in learning, but now it is time to ask again, are these changes for the better? Are we learning more than we used to? Or are we simply learning different things in different ways? As the Connecticon changes the external environment which we inhabit, and as it contributes to more effective, more efficient learning, will it also begin to change the basic capacity of the human brain to learn?

We have tried to explore both the benefits and the dangers of the changes. It is our view that these changes are evolutionary, but they are not evolving toward any knowable or necessarily "better" goal.

> Just as many early forecasts [of the change wrought by online learning] were overly optimistic, many later forecasts have failed to recognize real, albeit more evolutionary, transformations occurring already. (Dutton & Loader, 2002, p. 2)

We have sought to draw together these changes across a broad spectrum of what can be called "learning." We are not predicting revolution; we are documenting evolutionary change of a very profound and fundamental nature.

A more proactive stance in the face of the changes wrought by the Connecticon might be to say, where would we like these changes to lead us? How should the Connecticon be developed? What and how do we want learning to be in the future? At the broadest level, we want the Connecticon to be a support for human creativity in all its forms. In the last analysis, learning itself should be a means, not an end. The extent to which the components of the Connecticon can be directed, shaped or controlled, is very debatable. What we might aim for, however, are co-evolutionary paths in order that the benefits of connected learning outweigh the costs. We know that there is a mutual set of influences taking place such that the Internet shapes our behavior, and our behavior influences the development of the Internet.

In this chapter we will look at some of the more speculative developments of the Connecticon which will have long term effects on learning that we can only imagine from our current vantage point. These speculations center around:

- The urbanization of the Web.
- Connecting the virtual and the real.
- Personalization of learning.
- The future of universities.
- The Semantic Web.

THE URBANIZATION OF THE WEB

The last few centuries have seen the rise of physical cities as economic and social environments in which more and more people have chosen to live and work. This century is witnessing another kind of urbanization—the virtual world of the Internet, where millions of learners, consumers, and socializers congregate to engage in interactions of all sorts. Complex cyber-infrastructures in the form of large, complex portals have become centers of business transactions, information exchange, personal investigations and social activity. People are spending more and more of their time online searching for information, extracting ideas, entertaining themselves and building networks of social, economic and political activity.

> It's not difficult to imagine an environment in the next 10 to 20 years where the boundaries between the physical and the virtual worlds and our experience there either vanish or blend harmoniously to provide a new form of virtual urbanization. (Sairamesh, Lee, & Anania, 2004, p. 3)

eBay for example is a virtual city in its own right, and portals like yahoo and AOL's Digital Cities could be called super cities, attracting millions of users extracting knowledge, collaborating, buying, selling, socializing and transacting business every day. Ordinary life is being inextricably intertwined with the Internet as both are the focus for learning, socializing, working, and consuming.

As we have explored, the Net already offers numerous examples of organized social interaction, including hundreds of thousands of interacting groups supported by applications such as Usenet, listservs, AOL forums, multiuser domains (MUDs), Web-based discussions, and instant messaging. Information city designers must design for social interaction as well as for information consumption. In fact, participation in electronic communities often begins with a search for information.

> People certainly report receiving information benefits from their participation [in online communities], including facts, solutions to problems, learning, and insight. These benefits are derived from personalized information, rather than the depersonalized or authoritative information found in official databases and documents. One member of an electronic support group for people with hearing loss said, "It's one thing to visit a Web site or read about hearing issues. It's something quite different to read words composed by individuals with hearing impairments who aren't professional writers and not motivated by profit." (Sproull & Patterson, 2004, p. 34)

Furthermore, these researchers go on to point out that active participation begets more benefits as others are, in turn, motivated to participate, whereas people merely consuming information without participating themselves derive only limited benefit.

Information cities are not limited by physical boundaries and many American virtual cities boast millions of "inhabitants." The virtual city of Boston for example, has a 3D view of the real city offering information navigation and access. It is also beginning to integrate emergency response, health alerts and simulated training for fire departments and other emergency response units, along with ecommerce, shopping and social activities. An information city mixes eschooling, health and government services, edutainment and other learning centers with commercial suppliers, buyers, traders and regulators.

> We also envision many such information cities simultaneously promoting themselves to consumers with a range of competing services. More than one such information city will likely compete for and offer a range of services to residents of the same physical city; we thus expect them to turn to some form of specialization in order to serve the same consumer population. (Ferguson, Sairamesh, & Feldman, 2004, p. 47)

The vision here is of a full-scale urban existence taking place online. These researchers go on to speculate about schools and universities offering classes and lectures through the virtual city. Students register and pay through secure links, access their courses from home, hear the lectures as often as they like and discuss the contents with the lecturer and other students.

> All this means we can expect a new kind of virtual urbanization, where people spend more and more of their lives socializing and engaging in economic and political activities. We expect them to take many flavours, forms and spe-

cializations, while offering services involving social interaction, business transactions, municipal services, and daily commerce. Better user interfaces, mechanisms for ensuring trust and security, easy-to-use environments, social computing, and services for collaboration and communication are all aspects of the technology needed to produce stable information cities for everyone's benefit. (Sairamesh et al., 2004, p. 31)

Of course many people will object to this vision of the future, saying that face-to-face education continues to be preferred by students, and that virtual interaction will never substitute completely for real presence. Nevertheless, this virtual urbanization is happening right now, and so is a lot of virtual education. It is all a question of degree.

CONNECTING THE VIRTUAL AND THE REAL

There is evidence that people respond positively to the blurring of the boundary between online and offline realities and considerable research is devoted to applications which bring these two worlds more closely together (e.g., Churchill, Girgensohn, Nelson, & Lee, 2004)). Hewlett-Packard has systematically integrated Web services to enhance communications with mobile people, to provide location-specific services in the places that they visit and to provide interaction with the things that they encounter:

Most of our work has focused on extending Web technology, wireless networks, and portable devices to create a virtual bridge between mobile users and physical entities and electronic services. We think the physical world and the virtual world would both be richer if they were more closely linked. Currently the Web is largely a virtual space: a space of Web sites, online malls, and chat rooms. These virtual locations have little correspondence with physical spaces. While much of the information on the Web describes the world we physically inhabit, there are few systematic linkages to real world entities. This is unfortunate, because most of our activities concern physical objects other than computers. (Kindberg et al., 2003, p. 1)

Churchill et al. argue that blurring the notional boundary between the digital and the physical in social activity spaces helps blend—and motivate—online and face-to-face community participation. In their research, they developed an engaging online community space using large screen, interactive displays which they put in communal areas at a conference.

In bringing the content of online, digital community spaces directly into physical places, we intentionally invert the logic of virtual environment construction, which historically has involved representing real physical objects within digital spaces. (Churchill et al., 2004, p. 41)

The Connecticon has seen the blurring of other boundaries, as we have discussed in previous chapters. In particular, the boundary between learning and work, between formal and informal learning, and between learning and entertainment. We are already beginning to experience more and more of the online world impinging on and interacting on the physical world, with wearable computers, chips in common objects, and wireless communication everywhere. The days of thinking about the Internet as a separate sociotechnical system are past. The Internet has become embedded in the daily lives of much of the developed world. The always-on facility of broadband embeds the Internet heavily into everyday life; it is not necessary to make a special ritual of signing onto the Internet. One study showed that people valued such connectivity more than sheer speed. They could share a thought with their virtual friend as easily as with a co-located friend (Hampton & Wellman, 1999). One effect of the integration of the virtual and the real is the "everywhere/nowhere phenomenon." Communication can be from anywhere, but because it is independent of place, it is situated nowhere (Randall, 2001, p. 5). This is one component of what Wellman et al. call the rise of networked individualism.

> Each person is a switchboard, between ties and networks. People remain connected, but as individuals, rather than being rooted in the home bases of work unit and household. Each person operates a separate personal community network, and switches rapidly among multiple sub-networks. . . . In effect, the Internet and other new communication technology are helping each individual to personalize his or her own community. This is neither a prima facie loss nor gain in community, but rather a complex, fundamental transformation in the nature of community. (Wellman et al., 2003, p. 17)

What impact will this networked individualism and blurring of the real and virtual have on us as learners? The most obvious impact will be a further eroding of the boundary between formal and informal learning. Structured learning such as is found in books and lectures will not disappear, but simply be more mobile, flexible and independent of the classroom. Other predictions are that the student mindset will not regard the computer as technology, will not regard reality as real, will consider multitasking to be a way of life, and will not distinguish between consumer and creator (Frand, 2000). As was the case with broadband studies in the community, those who have experience of "laptop university" are quick to say that something intangible seems to happen when the technology is always available. The next "new thing" in teaching and technology may not emerge from the technology at all, but rather from how we, as active biological agents weave the technology into the fabric of our institutions, reframing the fundamental questions underlying why and how we teach (Long, 2002, p. 50).

THE PERSONALIZATION OF LEARNING

One of the promises made by futurologists of education is that the Connecticon will provide greater personalization of learning. The term has a variety of meanings and is sometimes used synonymously with customization. Most users agree that personalization involves a process of gathering user-information during interaction with the user. This is then used to deliver appropriate content and services, tailor-made to the user's needs. The aim is to improve the user's experience of a service. Customization occurs when the user can configure an interface and create a profile manually, adding and removing elements in the profile. The control of the look and content is explicit and is user-driven; that is, the user is involved actively in the process and has control. In personalization, on the other hand, the user is seen as passive, or at least somewhat less in control. It is the website that monitors, analyses and reacts to behavior (Bonett, 2001). The ecommerce applications of personalization are extensive. Amazon is a classic example: Amazon makes suggestions for products that should be of interest to the customer while they are browsing the site. It determines the user's interests from previous purchases as well as ratings given to titles. It then compares the user's interests with those of other customers to generate titles which are recommended to the user during interaction. Another example from the library and information field is the Personal Information Environment, sponsored by the Electronic Libraries program of the UK Higher Education Joint Information Systems Committee. Users can group favorite or most used resources from many pages. They can also change the look and feel of the page, and add their own logo and branding, and customize the pages at institutional level.[1] A similar project funded by the European Union developed a digital library infrastructure to support the communication and collaboration within networked scholarly communities. The project investigated how to provide personalized information dissemination to users by alerting them when new information, corresponding to a profile that they had created, became available.[2]

Cookies are another tool useful for personalization.

> The cookie is a small data packet sent by a Web site and stored on the browser side, that can be re-used on the server-side (the website that sent the cookie) as a unique identifier for a user. Cookies provide a means of tracing users. They can "tag" the user, or rather the user's browser files, so that the browser can be identified as a unique entity every time a return visit is made to the site that issued the cookie. (Bonett, 2001, p. 8)

The long term aim of personalized learning is that two learners could be accessing the same teaching material but see different presentations, and progress differently and satisfactorily.

> Personalization includes using learner-specific strategies that may take many forms as it adapts environments and offers alternative choices, including sequencing or presentation of content, practice, feedback, and assessment. Good instructors have been offering these personalization strategies in classrooms for years. In online learning situations, technology should ensure that these same strategies can be applied and increasingly self-managed by the online learners over time. (Martinez, 2002)

As an example of personalization, learners might choose to use an audio option because they prefer hearing text rather than reading it. Or a learner might prefer the presentation of content in a linear fashion rather than in hyperlinks. The learning experience may also be tailored to accommodate those with learning disabilities or may augment the traditional instruction by providing opportunities to explore a subject in greater depth. With personalized learning, the learning experience is no longer bounded by the length of the lecture or class session. This type of personalization works by collecting data, monitoring learning activity, comparing that activity with other learner behavior, and predicting what the user would like to do or see next.

With personalization, the tightly scripted, classroom-centered, seat-based form of instruction is challenged, and the new role for the lecturer is more like a coach. While this transition has already happened in distance education and its online equivalent, the predictions are that we will see this spread to campus-based education.

> The anytime, anyplace nature of this new set of electronic educational opportunities may well have its greatest impact on residential education. (Oblinger, Barone, & Hawkins, 2001, p. 1)

The same is true in the workplace, where personalized learning will look different in every organization, but at the core will be user-driven, user-directed learning that is available on demand. The learning goal is to develop employees who are able to:

- Be more responsive to changing business demand.
- Be able to innovate on demand.
- Derive more value from learning by integrating it with business process and systems.

For example, personalized workplace learning should include access to experts, best-practice databases, short elearning modules and simulations specifically related to the issue at hand.

Like virtual cities, personalization is a reality, though to a lesser degree in education than in commercial websites. The extent to which it is adopted in formal education remains to be seen—it requires extensive planning and course design, a student-centered pedagogy and a certain up-front investment to develop.

THE FUTURE OF UNIVERSITIES

There is a real paradox about the current state of universities in the western world. We have seen throughout the book, that individuals are seeking and finding all sorts of satisfying learning experiences through the various attributes of the Connecticon. Yet universities are finding it very difficult to capitalize on the obvious educational potential of the Connecticon and the aspirations and existing IT expertise of their learners. In short, the Connecticon has not had the impact on formal learning that had been forecast.

One large research project funded by the UK's Economic and Social Research Council concluded:

> The universities which we have studied have found the introduction of new technologies, alongside their more traditional methods of providing teaching and learning, extremely difficult and that the actual model of Virtual University which we have seen emerging bears little relationship to the vision. What we have found is that the Virtual University works in theory but not in practice. (Pollock & Cornfeld, 2000)

The editors of a whole collection of articles on The Digital Academe, note that:

> Even when individual educators embrace new technology, there are many institutional arrangements and policies in education that constrain more innovative uses of ICTs. For example, the incentive structures in most higher educational institutions continue to reward narrow definitions of scholarship, thereby failing to encourage work with new media—such as in authoring or collaborating on the development of educational software—or in reaching new audiences like life-long learners. (Dutton & Loader, 2002, p. 21)

Of course the sorts of people and examples we have highlighted in the book are not representative of the population as a whole. Some people are naturally more self-directed, more curious, more confident in seeking their own solutions and learning opportunities. There is anecdotal evidence that such people exist in all ages and strata of society. It is by no means an attribute of the young. The Connecticon certainly empowers such people, but what does it do for people without such natural instincts? Surely one of the many responsibilities of the university is to nurture this ability to elearn in all its learners. One American University President agrees:

> For decades, the trend in both pedagogy and scientific research was special-
> ization—knowing more and more about increasingly focused and more spe-
> cialized areas. Today the boundaries of specialization are blurring, just as the
> newer "threats" are becoming borderless. We have a responsibility to take our
> young people beyond the boundaries—national as well as disciplinary. We
> must answer simultaneously the questions concerning how to conduct scien-
> tific research and why it is important. (Jackson, 2004, p. 12)

She goes on to promote experiential learning as the pedagogy which
young people are seeking and which the Web facilitates. Interactive, experiential learning enhances cognition and analytical abilities, especially
when supported by teachers taking a mentoring role.

Commenting on the future of universities, Newton Smith observes:

> Virtually every academic discipline is perceived differently because of the
> Internet and the information available through computers. The content, the
> principles, and even the very facts of what we have traditionally taught are
> now seen as merely nodes or points in a network of an expanding, intercon-
> nected Web of information growing at an exponential rate. . . . This expan-
> sion of information has shaken our traditional concepts of knowledge.
> Everything that is passed to students as knowledge is temporary and subject
> to revision. (Smith, 2002, p. 40)

This new role for both learners and teachers reflects the fact that one of
the major impacts of the Connecticon is to blur the distinctions between
the producers and consumers of information. In terms of universities, this
has led to the rise of new actors in the higher education scene and new
providers of training and education. Another phenomenon is the networking amongst educational institutions to form new entities such as educational portals and consortia. The existing boundaries around educational
institutions are being eroded or blurred as they react to the pressures and
changes of the Connecticon.

THE SEMANTIC WEB

We have rapidly become accustomed to a network in which search engines
provide potential hits numbering in the thousands for many relevant and
important terms. Daily more than tens of thousands of Web pages of information are added to the net. One of the promises of The Semantic Web is
the development of nonhuman autonomous agents which will help augment our information retrieval and processing power. The "Semantic Web"
is a term coined by Tim Berners-Lee, founder of the Web, to refer to a
vision of a dramatic evolution of Web technology. He envisions forms of

intelligence and meaning being added to the display and navigational context of the current Web. The Semantic Web is a long-range development that is being built in stages by groups of researchers, developers, scientists and engineers around the world through a process of prototypes.

> The essential property of the World Wide Web is its universality. The power of a hypertext link is that "anything can link to anything." Web technology, therefore, must not discriminate between the scribbled draft and the polished performance, between commercial and academic information, or among cultures, languages, media and so on. Information varies along many axes. One of these is the difference between information produced primarily for human consumption and that produced mainly for machines. At one end of the scale we have everything from the five-second TV commercial to poetry. At the other end we have databases, programs and sensor output. To date, the Web has developed most rapidly as a medium of documents for people rather than for data and information that can be processed automatically. The Semantic Web aims to make up for this. (Berners-Lee, Hendler, & Lassila, 2001)

One of the challenges which The Semantic Web aims to address is to manipulate and organize the vast amounts of material on the Web, by allowing content to become aware of itself. Through the use of metadata organized in numerous interrelated ontologies, information is tagged with descriptors that facilitate its retrieval, analysis, processing and reconfiguration.

> The capacity of the Semantic Web to add meaning to information, stored such that it can be searched and processed, provides greatly expanded opportunities for education, simulation and real-time action anywhere on the distributed network. Critics have argued that the creation of a single network of semantically related mark-up is foolishly ambitious, and unworkable beyond small and centrally coordinated communities—a characteristic that is anathema to the current Web. Work in this area requires the development of appropriately scaled ontologies, systems that relate different ontologies to each other and systems that learn and mine ontology connections through use and the development of working prototype systems. (Anderson & Whitelock, 2004)

The challenge of tagging everything on the Internet into a coherent schema is immense and requires systems that allow tags to be acquired through use that allow multiple tags to describe the same data and systems that harvest and capture schema and tagging systems automatically. Thus, the Semantic Web is described and defended as a multi-year, if not a multi-decade, project.

The Semantic Web, in naming every concept simply by a URI, lets anyone express new concepts that they invent with minimal effort. Its unifying logical language will enable these concepts to be progressively linked into a universal Web. This structure will open up the knowledge and workings of humankind to meaningful analysis by software agents, providing a new class of tools by which we can live, work and learn together. (Berners-Lee et al., 2001)

What The Semantic Web promises is as significant for learning as The Connecticon is now. It remains to be seen whether this vision can be realized.

CONCLUSION

We have coined a term, the Connecticon, as a way of encompassing in one word, a range of concepts, technologies and practices. We have looked at a range of ways in which the term applies to learning. To a large extent our findings are consonant with those from the long and extensive Virtual Society? research project in the UK. Its conclusions have revealed the following:

- The uptake and use of the technologies depend crucially on local social context.
- The fears and risks associated with new technologies are unevenly socially distributed.
- Virtual technologies supplement rather than substitute for real activities.
- The more virtual, the more real.
- The more global, the more local (Macevièiûtë, 2003).

In short, there is considerable paradox in the way that the Connecticon is unfolding.

Our core assumptions about learning will have been apparent throughout the book, but we think they provide a fitting summary of what we have tried to convey.

First of all, learning is a continuous process that takes place throughout our lives as we try to make sense of the world. Learning is inextricably bound up in our experience and cannot be separated from activity. This is why experiential learning and problem-based approaches to teaching are so effective. Learning is driven by our own problems and questions—our desire to know.

Second, in order for knowledge to become truly our own, we need to assimilate it into our own way of thinking and relate it to our existing knowledge. Though this is ultimately a private and personal process, learning is in fact, socially mediated. Discussion in groups, team projects, and opportunities to compare one's understanding with that of others, all influence our appetite for learning and our confidence in what we know. Communities of practice provide the environment for us to negotiate meaning and to tackle larger problems.

Finally, the process of learning has to be a personal step. Although the teacher can do many things to enable learning to take place, learners must engage with the subject or problem, must direct their own learning and ultimately connect with the transforming power of knowing.

NOTES

1.   For details see, www.headline.ac.uk
2.   http://www.ercim.org/scholnet/

References

Abrioux, D. (2003). Interview with Dr. Dominique Abrioux. In *The future of e-learning: Realities, myths, challenges and opportunities*. Contact North Roundtable on e-Learning, Contact North, Thunder Bay, Ontario.

Adams, F. (1972). Highlander Folk School: Getting information, going back and teaching it. *Harvard Educational Review, 42*(4), 497–520.

Adelsberger, H., Collis, B., & Pawlowski, J. (Eds.). (2002). *Handbook on information technologies for education and training*. Berlin: Springer.

Alakeson, V., Aldrich, T., Goodman, J., & Jorgenson, B. (2003). *Making the net work: Sustainable development in a digital society*. Teddington: Xeris Publishing Company.

Allen, J.C. (1993). Development in a community under stress. *Community Development Journal, 28*(2), 154–66.

Allen, J.C., & Dillman, D.A. (1994). *Against all odds: Rural community in the information age*. Boulder, CO: Westview Press.

Alliance for Childhood. (1999). *Fool's gold: A critical look at computers in childhood*. Retrieved online 23/05/03. http://www.allianceforchildhood.net/projects/computers/computers_reports_fools_gold_intro.htm

Anderson, T., & Whitelock, D. (Eds.). (2004). Special Issue on The Semantic Web. *JIME*, April 2004. Retrieved online 29/04/04. http://www-jime.open.ac.uk/2004/1/

Andrews, D.C. (2002). Audience-specific online community design. *Communications of the ACM, 45*(4), 64–68.

Anthes, G (2001). Symbiotic intelligence. *ComputerWorld*, October 22, 2001. Retrieved online 29/03/04. http://www.computerworld.com/management-topics/management/story/0,10801,64912,00.html

Ascherson, N. (2003, Spring). Designing virtual citizens: Some Scottish experiments with electronic democracy. *Scottish Affairs, 43*.

The Connecticon: Learning for the Connected Generation, pages 157–169
Copyright © 2004 by Information Age Publishing

Bajan, P. (1998). New communities, new social norms? *Studia Psychologia, 40*(4), 361–366.

Bell, B., Gaventa, J., & Peters, J. (Eds.). (1990). *We make the road by walking: Conversations on education and social change: Myles Horton and Paulo Freire.* Philadelphia: Temple University Press.

Bennahum, D.S. (1998*). Into the matrix.* Retrieved online 23/02/04. http://memex.org/welcome.html

Bernath, U., Kleinschmidt, A., Walti, C., Zawacki, O., & von Ossietzky, C. (2003). Challenges for study centres in an electronic age: A case study of the Center for Distance Education at Carl von Ossietzky University of Oldenburgh in Germany. *International Review of Research in Open and Distance Learning, 4*(1). Retrieved online 05/06/03. http://www.irrodl.org/content/v4.1/bernath_etal.html

Berners-Lee, T., Hendler, J., & Lassila, O. (2001). The semantic web. *Scientific American*, May 2001. Retrieved online 28/03/04. http://www.sciam.com/article.cfm?articleID=00048144-10D2-1C70-84A9809EC588EF21

Billett, S. (2001). *Participation and continuity at work: A critique of current workplace learning discourses.* Paper given at the conference *Context, Power and Perspective: Confronting the Challenges to Improving Attainment in Learning at Work,* Sunley Management Centre, University College Northampton.

Birdsall, W.F. (1999). Policy and participation on the Canadian Information Highway. *First Monday, 4*(3). Retrieved online 06/07/03. http://www.firstmonday.dk/issues/issue4_3/birdsall/index.html

Birkerts, S. (1994). *The Gutenberg Elegies. The fate of reading in an electronic age.* New York: Fawcett Columbine.

Blackmore, S. (1999). *The meme machine.* Oxford: Oxford University Press.

Blacksburg. (2002). *Blacksburg Electronic Village home page.* Retrieved online 29/03/02. http://www.bev.net/

Blanchard, A., & Horan, T. (1998). Virtual communities and social capital. *Social Science Review, 16*(3), 293–307.

Bonett, M. (2001). Personalization of web services: Opportunities and challenges, *Ariadne, 28.* Retrieved online 28/03/04. http://www.ariadne.ac.uk/issue28/personalization/intro.html

Boud, D. (1995). Assessment and learning: Contradictory or complementary? In P. Knight (Ed.), *Assessment for learning in higher education.* London: Kogan Page.

Boyd, J. (2002). In community we trust: Online security communication at eBay. *Journal of Computer- Mediated Communication, 7*(3). Retrieved online 14/06/02. http://www.ascusc.org/jcmc/vol7/issue3/boyd.html

Brown, J.S. (2000, March/April). Growing up digital: How the web changes work, education, and the ways people learn. *Change,* pp .11–20. Retrieved online 17/12/03. http://www.aahe.org/change/digital.pdf

Bruckman, A. (2002). The future of e-learning communities. *Communications of the ACM, 45*(4), 60–63.

Bruffee, K.A. (1993). Education as conversation. In *Collaborative learning: Higher education, interdependence, and authority of knowledge.* Baltimore, MD: Johns Hopkins University Press.

Bryden, J., Black, S., & Rennie, F. (1993). *Final report on the evaluation of the Community Teleservice Centres in the Highlands and Islands.* The Arkleton Trust (Research) report to Highlands and Islands Enterprise.

BT. (2003). *Welcome to BT Openworld Broadband.* Retrieved online 13/05/03. http://btopenworld.com/broadband

Burbules, N.C. (2001). Like a Version: Playing with Online identities. Retrieved online 23/05/03. http://faculty.ed.uiuc.edu/burbules/ncb/papers/dreyfus.html

Calico UK. (2003). *Calico UK Internet services.* Retrieved online 14/05/03. http://www.cali.co.uk/

Carey, T. (2001). *The co-operative learnware object exchange.* Retrieved online 28/03/04. http://cloe.on.ac.CLOESummary.doc

Carey, T. (2003). Interview with Dr. Tom Carey. In *The future of e-learning: Realities, myths, challenges and opportunities.* Contact North Roundtable on e-Learning, Contact North, Thunder Bay, Ontario.

Carnet (Cambridge Ring Northeast). (2003). *Welcome to Cambridge Ring Northeast Project.* Retrieved online 14/05/03. http://www.carnet.uk.net/

Carroll, J.M., & Rosson, M.B. (1996, December). Developing the Blacksburg electronic village. *Communications of the ACM, 39*(12), 69–74.

Castells, M. (2001). *The internet galaxy.* Oxford: Oxford University Press.

Churchill, E., Girgensohn, A., Nelson, L., & Lee, A. (2004). Blending digital and physical spaces for ubiquitous community participation. *Communications of the ACM, 47*(2), 28–55.

Clark, D. (2003a). *Motivation and learning* (Epic Group White Paper). Retrieved 28/03/04. http://www.epic.co.uk

Clark, D. (2003b). *Blended learning* (Epic White Paper). Retrieved 10/10/03. http://www.epic.co.uk

Cleveland, H. (1985, January/February). The twilight of hierarchy: Speculations on the global information society. *Public Administration Review,* pp. 185–195.

Coatta, T. (2002). *Silicon chalk and pervasive learning.* Retrieved online 03/09/03. www.silicon-chalk.com/Documentation/White-Paper-Day-in-Life.pdf

Cobb, J.B. (1996). Defining normative community. In W. Vitek & W. Jackson (Eds.), *Rooted in the Land: Essays on community and place.* New Haven & London: Yale University Press.

Cohill, A.M. (2000). *Networks and the knowledge democracy: Nine challenges for communities.* Retrieved online 30/07/03. http://www.bev.net/about/research/digital_library/docs/cn_kd.pdf

Cohill, A.M. (2002). *Community networks: A web of relationships.* Retrieved online 21/08/03. http://www.bev.net/about/research/digital_library/docs/CNrelati.pdf

Cohill, A.M., & Kavanaugh, A.L. (Eds.) (2000). *Community networks: Lessons from Blacksburg, Virginia* (2nd ed.). London: Artech House.

Colley, H., Hodkinson, P., & Malcolm, J. (2002). *Non-formal learning: mapping the conceptual terrain.* A consultation report. Retrieved online 28/03/04. www.infed.org/archives/e-texts/colley_informal_learning.htm

Collis, B., De Boer, W.F., & Van der Veen, J.T. (2002). Building on learner contributions: A Web-supported pedagogic strategy. *Educational Media International, 38*(4), 229–240.

Coomey, M., & Stephenson, J. (2001). Online learning: It is all about dialogue, involvement, support and control—according to research. In J. Stephenson (Ed.), *Teaching and learning online. Pedagogies for new technologies*. London: Kogan Page.

Cross, J. (2003). Informal learning—The other 80%. Internet Time Group. Retrieved 19/08/04 from http://www.internettime.com/Learning/The%20 Other%2080%25.htm.

Cummings, J., Bonk, C., & Jacobs, F. (2002). Twenty-first century syllabi. Options for online communication and interactivity. *The Internet and Higher Education, 5*(1), 1–19.

Cunningham, S., Tapsall, S., Ryan, Y. Stedman, L., Bagdon, K., & Flew, T. (1998). *New media and borderless education*. Department of Employment, Education, Training, and Youth Affairs. Commonwealth of Australia.

Dabinett, G. (2000). Regenerating communities in the UK: getting plugged into the information society. *Community Development Journal, 35*(2), 157–166.

Daniel, J. (2002). Preface. In C. Vrasidas & G. Glass (Eds.), *Distance education and distributed learning*. Greenwich, CT: Information Age Publishing.

Davenport, T.H. (2001, Summer). eLearning and the attention economy: Here, there, and everywhere. *Line Zine*. Retrieved online 23/05/03. http://www.linezine.com/5.2/articles/tdeatae.htm

Davis, R., & Miller, L. (1999). Net empowering patients. *USA Today*, pp. 1A–2A.

Dawkins, R. (1978). *The selfish gene*. London: Paladin.

Day, G., & Murdoch, J. (1993). Locality and community: Coming to terms with place. *The Sociological Review*, pp. 82–111.

Dennett, D.C. (2003). *Freedom evolves*. London: Allen Lane/Penguin.

Dhesi, A. S. (2000). Social capital and community development. *Community Development Journal, 35*(3), 199–214.

Diamond, D. (2003). MIT everywhere. *Wired*, 11.09, Sept. 2003. Retrieved online 28/03/04. http://www.wired.com/wired/archive/11.09/mit.html

Downes, S. (1999). Hacking memes. *First Monday, 4*(10). Retrieved online 6/06/03. http://www.firstmonday.dk/issues/issue4_10/downes

Downes, S. (2003). Interview with Stephen Downes. In *The future of e-learning: Realities, myths, challenges and opportunities*. Contact North Roundtable on e-Learning, Contact North, Thunder Bay, Ontario.

Duncan, C., & Ekmekcioglu, C. (2003). Digital libraries and repositories. In A. Littlejohn (Ed.), *Reusing online resources: A sustainable approach to e-learning*. London: Kogan Page.

Dutton, W., & Loader, B. (Eds.). (2002). *Digital academe*. London: Routledge.

Edwards, R., & Usher, R. (2000). *Globalisation and pedagogy. Space, place and identity*. London: Routledge/Falmer.

e-fro. (2003). *e-fro: Developing the communities of Wales through wireless broadband*. Retrieved online 13/05/03. http://www.e-fro.cd/en/

Ehrenfeld, D. (1996). Pseudocommunities. In W. Vitek, & W. Jackson (Eds.), *Rooted in the land: Essays on community and place*. New Haven & London: Yale University Press.

Eraut, M. (2000). Non-formal learning, implicit learning and tacit knowledge. In F. Coffield (Ed.) *The necessity of informal learning*. Bristol: Policy Press.

Erickson, T., Halverson, C., Kellogg, W. A., Laff, M., & Wolf, T. (2002). Social translucence: Designing social infrastructures that make collective activity visible. *Communications of the ACM, 45*(4), 40–44.

Etzioni, A., & Etzioni, O. (1999). Face-to-face and computer-mediated communities, a comparative analysis. *Information Society, 15*(4), 241–248.

European Commission. (2001). *Communication: Making a European area of lifelong learning a reality.* Retrieved online 28/03/04. http://www.european.int/comm/education/life/index.htm

Evans, F. (2000). Cyberspace and the concept of democracy. *First Monday, 5*(10). Retrieved online 06/06/03. http://www.firstmonday.dk/issues/issue5_10/evans/index.html

Ewell, P. (1997). Organizing for learning. A new imperative. *AAHE Bulletin,* American Association for Higher Education. Retrieved online 04/07/03. http://aahebulletin.com/member/articles/organizingewell.asp?pf=1

Falk, I., & Kilpatrick, S. (2000, January). What is social capital? A study of interaction in rural community. *Sociologia Ruralis, 40*(1), 88–110.

Ferguson, D., Sairamesh, J., & Feldman, S. (2004). Open Frameworks for Information Cities. *Communications of the ACM, 47*(2), 28–55.

Fox, N., & Roberts, C. (1999). GPs in cyberspace: The sociology of a "virtual community." *Sociological Review, 47*(4), 643–671.

Frand, J. (2000). The information age mindset: Changes in students and implications for higher education. *EDUCAUSE Review, 35*(5), 15–24.

Frank, J. (1999). Applying memetics to financial markets: Do markets evolve towards efficiency? *Journal of Memetics—Evolutionary Models of Information Transmission, 3.* Retrieved online 17/12/03. http://jom-emit.cfpm.org/vol3/frank_j.html

Friesen, N. (2004). Three objections to learning objects. In R. McGreal (Ed.) *Online education using learning objects.* London: Taylor & Francis Books Ltd.

Gabora, L. (1997). The origin and evolution of culture and creativity. *Journal of Memetics—Evolutionary Models of Information Transmission, 1.* Retrieved online 17/12/03. http://jom-emit.cfpm.org/vol1/gabora_1.html

Garnham, N. (2002). Information society as theory or ideology: A critical perspective on technology, education and employment in the information age. In W. Dutton & B. Loader (Eds.), *Digital academe.* London: Routledge.

Garret, R. (2003, February). Mapping the education industry. *Observatory on Borderless Higher Education,* Issue 12. Retrieved online 01/06/03. http://www.obhe.ac.uk/products/reports/pdf/February2003.pdf

Gibbons, M., Limoges, C., Nowotny, H., Schwartzman, S., Scott, P., & Trow, M. (1994). *The new production of knowledge.* London: Sage.

Gilchrist, A. (2000). The well-connected community: Networking to the "edge of chaos." *Community Development Journal 35*(3), 264–275.

Gitta, S., & Ikoja-Odongo, J.R. (2003). The impact of cybercafes on information services in Uganda. *First Monday, 8*(4). Retrieved online 27/06/03. http://www.firstmonday.dk/issues/issue8_4/gitta/index.html

Glen, J. (1988). Highlander: No ordinary school, 1932–1962. Lexington: University Press of Kentucky.

Glogoff, S. (2001). Virtual connections: Community bonding on the net. *First Monday*, 6(3). Retrieved online 05/03/02. http://www.firstmonday.dk/issues/issue6_3/glogoff/index.html

Goldhaber, M. (1998a). The attention economy will change everything. *Telepolis*. Retrieved online 27/05/03. http://www.heise.de/tp/english/inhalt/te/1419/1.html

Goldhaber, M.H. (1997, April). The attention economy and the net. *First Monday, 2* (4). Retrieved online 27/05/03. http://www.firstmonday.dk/issues/issue2_4/goldhaber/index.html

Goldhaber, M. (1998b). *M. H. Goldhaber's principles of the new economy.* Retrieved online 01/03/04. http://www.well.com/user/mgoldh/principles.html

Gomez, R., Hunt, P., & Lamoureux, E. (1999). *Enchanted by telecentres: A critical look at universal access to information technologies for international development.* Paper presented at the conference "New IT and Inequality," University of Maryland. Retrieved online 05/02/02. http://www.idrc.ca/pan/enchanted.html

Gongla, P., & Rizzuto, C. R. (2001). Evolving communities of practice: IBM Global Services experience. *IBM Systems Journal, 40*(4), 842–862. Retrieved online 17/05/02. http://www.research.ibm.com/journal/sj/404/gongla.html

Gurstein, M. (1999, February). Flexible networking, information and communications technology and local economic development. *First Monday, 4*(2). Retrieved online 08/03/02. http://www.firstmonday.dk/issues/issue4_2/gurstein/index.html

Hake, R. (1998). Interactive engagement vs. traditional methods: A six thousand student survey of mechanics test data for introductory physics courses. *American Journal of Physics, 66,* 64–74.

Hampton, K., & Wellman, B. (1999). Netville on-line and off-line. *American Behavioral Scientist, 43*(3), 478–495.

Hanley, F. (2003). *Enabling educational institutions' success in distance learning:* MERLOT's Facilitation Strategy, International Symposium 2003 Networks without Borders, National Institute of Multimedia Education, Japan.

Harrison, M. (2003). *Blended learning II: Blended learning in practice* (Epic Group White Paper). Retrieved online 29/01/04. http://www.epic.co.uk

Haykin, S. (1999). *Neural networks: A comprehensive foundation* (2nd ed.). Engelwood Cliffs, NJ: Prentice-Hall.

Hillery, G.A. (1955). Definitions of community: Areas of agreement. *Rural Sociology, 2,* 111–123.

Hiltz, S.R., & Turoff, M. (2002). What makes learning networks effective? *Communications of the ACM, 45*(4), 56–59.

ITU (International Telecommunication Union). (1998). *The role of community telecentres in fostering universal access and rural development.* Regional Seminar for Central European Countries, Budapest, 7–9 December 1998. Retrieved online 12/08/03. http://www.itu.int/ITU-D/univ_access/seminar/buda/proceedings/Budapest-en.pdf

Jackson, S. (2004, January/February). Ahead of the curve. Future shifts in higher education. *Educause.*

Jonassen, D. (2002). Learning to solve problems online. In C. Vrasidas & G. Glass (Eds.), *Distance education and distributed learning.* Greenwich, CT: Information Age Publishing.

Jones, S. (2003). *Let the games begin: Gaming technology and entertainment among college students.* Retrieved online 28/03/04. http://www.pewinternet.org/reports/toc.asp?Report=93

Jordan, K., Hauser, J., & Foster, S. (2003). The augmented social network: Building identity and trust into the next generation Internet. *First Monday, 8*(8). Retrieved online 08/12/03. http://www.firstmonday.dk/issues/issue8_8/jordan/index.html

Kelly, K. (1997, September 17). New rules for the new economy. *Wired Magazine.* Retrieved online 23/05/03. http://www.wired.com/wired/archive/5.09/newrules_pr.html

Kemmis, D. (1996). Barn raising. In W. Vitek & W. Jackson (Eds.), *Rooted in the land: Essays on community and place.* New Haven & London: Yale University Press.

Kim, A.J. (2000). *Community building on the web: Secret strategies for successful online communities.* Berkeley, CA: Peachpit Press.

Kindberg, T., Barton, J., Morgan, J., Becker, G., Caswell, D., Debaty, P., Gopal, G., Frid, M., Krishnan, V., Morris, H., Schettino, J., & Serra, B. (2003). *People, places, things: Web presence for the real world.* Cooltown Research (Hewlett Packard). Retrieved online 17/12/03. http://www.cooltown.com/dev/wpapers/bartonppt.pdf

Kling, R. (1996). Synergies and competition between life in cyberspace and Face-to-face communities. *Social Science Computer Review, 14*(1), 50–54.

Koert, R. Van (2002, April). The impact of democratic deficits on electronic media in rural development. *First Monday, 7*(4). Retrieved online 31/05/03. http://www.firstmonday.dk/issues/issue7_4/koert/index.html

Koory, M. (2003). Differences in learning outcomes for the online and F2F versions of "an introduction to shakespeare." *JALN, 7*(2). Retrieved online 28/03/04. http://www.aln.org/publications/jaln/v7n2/v7n2_koory.asp

Kubey, R., Lavin, M., & Barrows, J. (2001). Internet use and collegiate academic performance decrements: early findings. *Journal of Communication, 51*(2), 366–382.

Kumari, D. (2001). Connecting graduate students to virtual guests through asynchronous discussions–Analysis of an experience. *JALN, 5*(2). Retrieved online 28/03/04. http://www.aln.org/publications/jaln/v5n2/v5n2_kumari.asp

Lanham, R. (1994). The economics of attention. *Proceedings of the 124th Annual Meeting, Association of Research Libraries.* Retrieved online 06/02/03. http://sunsite.berkeley.edu/ARL/Proceedings/124/ps2econ.html

Lankshear, C. (2003). The Challenge of Digital Epistemologies. *Education, Communication & Information, 3*(2), 167–186.

Lankshear, C., & Knobel, M. (2001). Do we have your attention? New literacies, digital technologies and the education of adolescents In D. Alvermann (Ed.), *New literacies and digital technologies: A focus on adolescent learners.* New York: Peter Lang. Retrieved online 23/05/03. http://www.geocities.com/c.lankshear/attention.html

Latchem, C., & Walker, D. (Eds.). (2001). *Telecentres: Case studies and key issues*. The Commonwealth of Learning, Retrieved online 12/08/03. http://www.col.org/telecentres/

Lave, J., & Wenger, E. (1990). *Situated learning: Legitimate peripheral participation*. Cambridge: Cambridge University Press.

Lewis, D. (1999). *Information overload: Practical strategies for surviving in today's workplace*. London: Penguin Books.

Littlejohn, A (Ed.). (2003). *Reusing online resources: A sustainable approach to e-learning*. London: Kogan Page.

Long, P. (2002, May/June). Needed: Creative teaching & commitment. *EDUCAUSE Review*.

Lynch, C. (2000, November). Why broadband really matters: Applications and architectural challenges. *Educause Quarterly*.

McDermott, R. (2000, November/December). Community development as a natural step: Five stages of community development. *KM Review, 3*(5).

Macevièiûtê, E. (2003). Review of *Virtual society? Technology, cyberbole, reality* [S. Woolgar, Ed., Oxford: Oxford University Press, 2002]. *Information Research, 9*(1), review no. R112 Retrieved online 28/03/04. http://informationr.net/ir/reviews/revs112.html

McGivney, V. (1999). *Informal learning in the community: A trigger for change and development*. NIACE, Leicester.

McGovern, G. (2003). *The intranet gets serious: Part 2: making knowledge sharing work*. Retrieved online 28/03/04. http://www.gerrymcgovern,com/nt/2003/nt_2003_11_2_intranet_2.htm

McGreal, R. (Ed.). (2004). *Online education using learning objects*. London: Taylor & Francis Books Ltd.

McInnes, A. (1997). The agency of the infozone: Exploring the effects of a community network. *First Monday, 2*(2). Retrieved online 14/03/02. http://www.firstmonday.dk/issues/issue2_2/mcinnes/index.html

MacLean, M., & Dorgan, T. (Eds.). (2002). *An Leabhar Mor: The great book of Gaelic*. Edinburgh: Canongate Books.

Manniche, J., & Marcussen, C.H. (1997). Telematics–opportunity of threat for peripheral areas? *Rural Society, 7*(3/4), 13–26. Retrieved online 26/09/02. http://www.csu.edu.au/research/crsr/ruralsoc/v7no34.pdf

Marathe, J. (1999). Creating community online. Retrieved online 24/04/02. http://www.durlacher.com/research/resrepdetail21.asp

Marchese, T. (1997). The new conversations about learning. *American Association for Higher Education*. Retrieved online 04/07/03. http://www.aahe.org/pubs/TM-essay.htm

Marten, G.G. (2001). *Human ecology: Basic concepts for sustainable development*. London: Earthscan.

Martinez, M. (2002). *Adaptive and personalized learning: The training place*. Retrieved online 28/03/04. http://trainingplace.com/source/research/masspersonalization.htm

Martocchio, J. (1992). Microcomputer usage as an opportunity: The influence of context in employee training, *Personnel Psychology, 45*, 529–551.

Mason, R. (1989). *A case study of the use of computer conferencing at the Open University.* Unpublished Ph.D. thesis, CITE, The Open University.

Mason, R. (1998). *Globalisation education: Trends and applications.* Routledge: London.

Mason, R., Pegler, C., & Weller, M. (in press). A learning object success story. (JALN).

Matthews, D., & Schrum, L. (2003). High-speed Internet use and academic gratifications in the college residence. *The Internet and Higher Education, 6,* 125–144.

Mayes, T. (2002). *Pedagogy, lifelong learning and ICT: A discussion paper for the Scottish Forum on Lifelong Learning.* Retrieved online 22/05/02. http://www.usq.edu.au/electpub/e-jist/html/full_papers.html

Millen, D.R., Fontaine, M.A., & Muller.,M.J. (2002). Understanding the benefit and costs of communities of practice. *Communications of the ACM, 45*(4), 69–73.

Milojicic, D.S. (2002). *Pervasive services infrastructure.* Hewlett Packard research web site. Retrieved online 05/03/04. http://www.hpl.hp.com/research/

Milojicic, D., Messer, A., Bernadat, P., Greenberg, D., Fu, G., Spinczyk, O., Beuche, D., & Schroder-Preikschat, W. (2002). *Pervasive services infrastructure.* Hewlett Packard research web site. Retrieved online 05/03/04. http://www.hpl.hp.com/research/

Mocker, D., & Spear, G. (1982). *Lifelong learning: Formal, nonformal, informal and self-directed.* ERIC Clearninghouse on Adult, Career, and Vocational Education, Information Series, No 241, Columbus, Ohio.

Morahan-Martin, J., & Schumacher, P. (2000). Incidence and correlates of pathological Internet use among college students. *Computers in Human Behavior, 16,* 13–29.

Morgan, A. (1993). *Improving your students' learning. Reflections on the experience of study.* London: Kogan Page.

Naidu, S. (2003). Designing instruction for e-learning environments. In M. Moore & W. Anderson (Eds.) *Handbook of distance education.* Hillsdale, NJ: Lawrence Erlbaum Associates.

Naidu, S., & Oliver, M. (1996). Computer supported collaborative problem-based learning (CSC-PBL): An instructional design architecture for virtual learning in nursing education. *Journal of Distance Education, XI*(2), 1–22.

Naidu, S., Ip, A., & Linser, R. (2000). Dynamic goal-based role-play simulation on the Web: A case study. *Educational Technology & Society, 3*(3). Retrieved online 28/03/04. http://ifets.ill.org/periodical/vol_3_2000/b05.html

Nardi, B.A., & O'Day, V.L. (1999). Information ecologies: Using technology with heart. *First Monday, 4*(5). Retrieved online 28/01/04. http://www.firstmonday.dk/issues/issue4_5/nardi_contents.html

Nardi, B.A., Whittaker, S., & Schwarz, H. (2000). It's not what you know, it's who you know: Work in the Information Age. *First Monday, 5*(5). Retrieved online 06/06/03. http://www.firstmonday.dk/issues/issue5_5/nardi/index.html

National Adult Learning Survey. (2001). Retrieved online 08/08/03. http://www.lifelonglearning.dfee.gov.uk/iln/late17.htm

National Research Council. (2002). Broadband. Bringing home the bits. Washington, DC: National Academy Press.

Negroponte, N. (1995). *Being digital.* London: Coronet Books.

Northcote, M., & Kendle, A. (2001). *Informal online networks for learning: Making use of incidental learning through recreation.* Retrieved online 28/03/04. http://www.aare.edu.au/01pap/nor01596.htm

Oblinger, D. (2003). Interview with Dr. Oblinger, *The future of e-learning,* Contact North Roundtable on e-Learning, Contact North, Thunder Bay, Ontario.

Oblinger, D. (2004, April). The next generation of educational engagement. *JIME.* Retrieved online 29/04/04. http://www-jime.open.ac.uk/2004/1/

Oblinger, D., Barone, C., & Hawkins, B. (2001). Distributed education and its challenges: An overview. *Educause.* Retrieved online 28/03/04. http://www.acenet.edu/bookstore

Odlyzko, A. (2003, September). The many paradoxes of broadband. *First Monday, 8*(9). Retrieved online 29/03/04. http://www.dtc.umn.edu/~odlyzko

Oksa, J. (2001). *How to be rural in information age: Case of rural community network in Finnish periphery.* Paper to the XIX Congress of the European Society for Rural Sociology. Retrieved online 05/02/02. http://cc.joensuu.fi/~alma/infosoc/dijonoksa.pdf

Oksa, J., & Turunen, J. (2000). *Local community net: Evaluation study of the learning Upper Karelia project.* Retrieved online 09/01/02. http://www.joensuu.fi/ktl/projsoc/infosoc/upperkar.htm

Oldenburg, R. (1995). *The great good place: Cafes, coffee shops, bookstores, bars, hair salons and other hangouts at the heart of a community.* New York: Marlowe & Company.

Oliver, R., & McLoughlin, C. (2003). Pedagogical designs for scalable and sustainable online learning. In A. Littlejohn (Ed.) *Reusing online resources: A sustainable approach to e-learning.* London: Kogan Page.

Owen, W., & Darkwa, O. (2000). Role of multipurpose community telecentres in accelerating national development in Ghana. *First Monday, 5*(1). Retrieved online 08/03/02. http://www.firstmonday.dk/issues/issues5_1/owen/index.html

Palloff, R., & Pratt, K. (1999). *Building learning communities in cyberspace. Effective strategies for the online classroom.* San Francisco: Jossey-Bass.

Parman, S. (1990). *Scottish crofters: A historical ethnography of a Celtic village.* London: Holt, Rinehart and Winston Inc.

PNE (Proiseact nan Ealain–The Gaelic Arts Development Agency). (2003). *An Leabhar Mor: The great book of Gaelic.* Retrieved online 08/05/03. http://www.leabharmor.net/

Pollock, N., & Cornford, J. (2000). Theory and practice of the virtual university. *Ariadne, 24.* Retrieved online 28/03/04. http://www.ariadne.ac.uk/issue24/virtual-universities/intro.html

Polsani, P. (2003). Use and abuse of reusable learning objects. *Journal of Digital Information, 3*(4). Retrieved online 28/03/04. http://jodi.ecs.soton.ac.uk/Articles/v03/i04/Polsani/

Portes, A. (1998). Social capital: Its origins and applications in modern sociology. *Annual Review of Sociology, 24*(1), 1–24.

Poster, M. (1990). *The mode of information. Poststructuralism and social context.* Cambridge: Polity Press.

Preece, J. (2000). *Online communities: Designing usability. supporting sociability.* Chichester: Wiley.

Preece, J. (2002). Supporting community and building social capital. *Communications of the ACM, 45*(4), 37–39.

Putnam, R.D. (1995). Bowling alone: America's declining social capital. *Journal of Democracy, 6*(1), 65–78.

Qvortrup, L. (1989, March). The Nordic telecottages: Community teleservice centres for rural regions. *Telecommunications Policy*, pp. 59–68.

Qvortrup, L. (1994). Community teleservice centres around the world. *Proceedings of the Irish Teleworking Conference, 1994.* Retrieved online 05/02/02. http://www.csu.edu.au/research/crsr/sai/community.htm

Radio Acen. (2003). Welcome to Radio Acen. Retrieved online 13/05/03. http://www.radioacen.fm/

Ramsden, P. (1992). *Learning to teach in higher education.* London: Routledge.

Randall, N. (2001, January 2). Stay in touch. *PC Magazine*, pp. 101–104.

Rehak, D., & Mason, R. (2003). Keeping the learning in learning objects. In A. Littlejohn (Ed.), *Reusing online resources: A sustainable approach to e-learning.* London: Kogan Page.

Rennie, F. (1987). *Popular education for change.* Report to the Arkleton Trust on a visit in April/May 1986 to The Highlander Research and Education Center, Tennessee. The Arkleton Trust: Enstone, UK.

Reynolds, J., Caley, L., & Mason, R. (2002). *How do people learn?* Chartered Institute of Personnel and Development Research Report. Retrieved online 28/03/04. http://www.cipd.co.uk/publications

Rheingold, H. (1994). *The virtual community HB: Surfing the internet.* Cambridge, MA: Perseus Publishing.

Rheingold, H. (2000). *The virtual community* (rev. ed.). Cambridge, MA: MIT Press. (2nd ed., 1998). Retrieved online 05/03/02. http://www.rheingold.com/vc/book

Rheingold, H. (2002). *Smart mobs: The next social revolution.* Cambridge, MA: Perseus Publishing.

Riedel, E., Dresel, L., Wagoner, M.J., Sullivan, J.L., & Borgida, E. (1998). Electronic communities: Assessing equality of access in a rural Minnesota community. *Social Science Computer Review 16*(4), 370–390.

Riley, P., Keough, C.M., Christiansen, T., Meilich, O., & Pierson, J. (1998). Community or colony: The case of online newspapers and the web. *Journal of Computer Mediated Communication, 4*(1). Retrieved online 14/06/02. http://www.ascusc.org/jcmc/vol4/issue1/keough.html

Rose, N. (1998). Controversies in meme theory. *Journal of Memetics–Evolutionary Models of Information Transmission, 2.* Retrieved online 18/04/03. http://jom-emit.cfpm.org/1998/vol2/rose_n.html

Sage Research. (2002). *Customers at the gate: Mounting demand for broadband-enabled services.* Natick, MA. Retrieved online 05/12/02. http://www.sageresearch.com/

Sairamesh, J., Lee, A., & Anania, L. (2004). Information cities. *Communications of the ACM, 47*(2), 28–55.

Sandler, J. (1999). *Telecentres in the Highlands and Islands: Was the CTC pilot programme a success?* Unpublished MSc dissertation to the University of Aberdeen.

Segrave, S., & Holt, D. (2003). Contemporary learning environments: Designing e-learning for education in the professions. *Distance Education, 24*(1), 7–24.

Selznick, P. (1996). In search of community. In W. Vitek & W. Jackson (Eds.), *Rooted in the land: Essays on community and place.* New Haven & London: Yale University Press.

Senge, P. (1990). *The fifth discipline. The art and practice of the learning organization.* New York: Bantam Doubleday Dell Publishing Group, Inc.

Share, P. (1993). Review Article: Telecommunications and rural and remote Australia. *Rural Society, 3*(3). Retrieved online 25/07/02. http://www.csu.edu.au/research/crsr/ruralsoc/v3n3p22.htm

Shenk, D. (1997). *Data smog: Surviving the information glut.* New York: Harper Collins.

Simpson, L., Daws, L., & Wood, L. (2003). More than just an Internet connection: Building rural social capital through public access. *Rural Society, 13*(2), 113–125.

Smith, M.A., & Kollock, P. (Eds.). (1999). *Communities in cyberspace.* London: Routledge.

Smith, M.K. (2002). *Andragogy: The history and current use of the term. The informal education homepage.* Retrieved online 22/05/02. http://www.infed.org/lifelonglearning/b-andra.htm

Smith, N. (2002, May/June). Teaching as coaching. *EDUCAUSE Review.* Retrieved online 29/03/04. http://www.educause.edu/pub/er/erm02/erm023.asp

Sproull, L., & Patterson, J. (2004). Making information cities liveable. *Communications of the ACM, 47*(2), 28–55.

Strategic Networks Group. (2003). *Economic Impact study of the South Dundas Township fibre network: Primary findings.* Retrieved online 29/03/04. http://www.sngroup.com

Streibel, M.J. (1998). Information technology and physicality in community, place, and presence. *Theory into Practice, 37*(1), 31–37.

Swan, K. (2002). Building learning communities in online courses: The importance of interaction. *Education, Communication, and Information, 2*(1), 23–49.

Szabo, M. (2002). Competencies for educators. In H. Adelsberger, B. Collis, & J. Pawlowski (Eds.), *Handbook on Information technologies for education and training.* Berlin: Springer.

Turkle, S. (1996). Virtuality and its discontents: Searching for community in cyberspace. *The American Prospect, 24*, 50–57.

UNESCO. (2002, July). *Forum on the impact of open courseware for higher education in developing countries.* UNESCO.

Vale, K., & Long, P. (2003). Models for open learning. In A. Littlejohn (Ed.), *Reusing online resources: A sustainable approach to e-learning.* London: Kogan Page.

Vincent, A., & Shepherd, J. (1998). Experiences in teaching Middle East politics via Internet-based role-play simulations. *Journal of Interactive Media in Education, 98*(11). Retrieved online 29/03/04. http://www-jime.open.ac.uk/98/11

Visser, J. (1997). *Multilingualism in a pervasive learning environment.* UNESCO Learning Without Frontiers Unit. Retrieved online 03/09/03. http://www.unesco.org/education/educprog/lwf/doc/multi.html

Watts, J. (2004, February 12–18). China tightens net around online dissenters. *Guardian Weekly,* p. 3.

Wellman, B., & Gulia, M. (1999). Virtual communities as communities: Net surfers don't ride alone. In M.A. Smith & P. Kollock (Eds.), *Communities in cyberspace.* London: Routledge.

Wellman, B., Quan-Haase, A., Boase, J., Chen, W., Hampton, K., Isla de Diaz, I., & Miyata, K. (2003). The social affordances of the internet for networked individualism. *JCMC, 8*(3). Retrieved online 29/03/04. http://www.ascusc.org/jcmc/vol8/issue3/wellman.html

Welsh Assembly Government. (2003). *Cymru Ar-lein: Online for a better Wales.* Retrieved online 13/05/03. http://www.cymruarlein.wales.gov.uk/broadband.htm

Wenger, E.C. (1998). Communities of practice: Learning as a social system. *Systems Thinker, 9*(5), 2–3.

Werry, C. (1999). Imagined electronic community: Representations of virtual community in contemporary business discourse. *First Monday, 4*(9). Retrieved online 29/03/04. http://www.firstmonday.dk/issues/issue4_9/werry/index.html

Wetterling, J., & Collis, B. (2003). Sharing and reuse of learning resources across a transnational network. In A. Littlejohn (Ed.), *Reusing online resources: A sustainable approach to e-learning.* London: Kogan Page.

Wiley, D. (2003). *Learning objects: Difficulties and opportunities.* Retrieved online 29/03/04. http://wiley.ed.usu.edu/docs/lo_do.pdf

Wilson, P.A. (1997). Building social capital: A learning agenda for the twenty-first century. *Urban Studies, 34*(5/6), 745–761.

World Bank. (2002). *Constructing knowledge societies: New challenges for tertiary education.* Washington, DC: World Bank.

Printed in the United States
29257LVS00001B/119-140

9 781593 112097